MISCHIEF   Matchmaker Merino DK

3

ALLURE
Matchmaker
Merino Aran

PEACE
Extra Fine
Merino DK

CLOVER
*Matchmaker
Merino DK*

PEACE   Matchmaker Merino DK

CALM
*Extra Fine
Merino DK*

DRIFT
Alpaca 4 ply

9

BLUSTER   Shetland Aran

STEVIE
Matchmaker
Merino 4 ply

PEACE
Matchmaker
Merino DK

HEART
Matchmaker
Merino 4 ply

TRAIL Matchmaker Merino Chunky   HUSH Matchmaker Merino Aran

WORTH
Cashmere 4 ply

BLUSTER   Matchmaker Merino Aran

MULL
Shetland Aran

CLOUD
Extra Fine
Merino DK

CHEVRON CUSHIONS
& MAPLE THROW

TRANQUILLITY   Matchmaker Merino 4 ply

VOYAGE Matchmaker Merino Chunky
& TRANQUILLITY Alpaca 4 ply

HEART
Matchmaker
Merino 4 ply

Autumn/Winter

Contents

Design 1

Tranquillity

To fit bust

| 81 | **86** | 91 | **97** | 102 | cm |
| 32 | **34** | 36 | **38** | 40 | in |

Actual size, at underarm
Sweater

| 86 | **92** | 98 | **104** | 109 | cm |
| 34 | **36** | 38¹/₂ | **41** | 43 | in |

Cardigan

| 91 | **96** | 102 | **108** | 114 | cm |
| 36 | **38** | 40 | **42¹/₂** | 45 | in |

Finished length
Sweater

| 46 | **46** | 47 | **47** | 48 | cm |
| 18 | **18** | 18¹/₂ | **18¹/₂** | 19 | in |

Cardigan

| 48 | **48** | 49 | **49** | 50 | cm |
| 19 | **19** | 19¹/₂ | **19¹/₂** | 19¹/₂ | in |

Sleeve length to underarm
Sweater

| 9 | **9** | 9 | **9** | 9 | cm |
| 3¹/₂ | **3¹/₂** | 3¹/₂ | **3¹/₂** | 3¹/₂ | in |

Cardigan

| 46 | **46** | 47 | **47** | 47 | cm |
| 18 | **18** | 18¹/₂ | **18¹/₂** | 18¹/₂ | in |

Jaeger Matchmaker Merino 4 ply
Sweater (693 and 716)

| 5 | **5** | 5 | **5** | 6 | 50 gm |

Cardigan (693 and 716)

| 6 | **6** | 7 | **7** | 8 | 50 gm |

Jaeger Cashmere 4 ply
Sweater

| 9 | **9** | 10 | **10** | 11 | 25 gm |

Cardigan

| 11 | **12** | 12 | **12** | 14 | 25 gm |

Jaeger Alpaca 4 ply
Sweater (384)

| 5 | **5** | 5 | **5** | 6 | 50 gm |

Cardigan

| 6 | **6** | 7 | **7** | 8 | 50 gm |

Quantities of yarn are approximate as they are based on average requirements. Check actual yarn colour - as printing may not match yarn exactly.

Matchmaker Merino and Cashmere 4 ply versions: Pair each of 2³/₄ mm (UK 12/USA 2) and 3¹/₄ mm (UK 10/USA 3) needles.
Alpaca 4 ply version: Pair each of 2¹/₄ mm (UK 13/USA 1) and 3 mm (UK 11/USA 2/3) needles.
Cardigan: 8 buttons.
Beaded versions: Approx 1,450 small glass beads for Sweater, and approx 2,100 small glass beads for Cardigan.

Tension
28 sts and 36 rows to 10 cm (stocking st) on larger size needles or size needed to achieve stated tension.

For notes and abbreviations, see page 58.

TEXTURED VERSIONS

SWEATER
BACK

With smaller size needles, cast on 103 [**111**, 119, **127**, 135] sts.
Rib row 1 - (RS), K1, *K1 tbl, P1; rep from * to last 2 sts, K1 tbl, K1.
Rib row 2 - K1, P1 tbl, *K1 tbl, P1 tbl; rep from * to last st, K1.
Rep these 2 rows for 6 cm, ending with row 2.
Change to larger size needles and **patt** thus:
Row 1 - (RS), Knit.
Row 2 and every foll alt row - Purl.
Row 3 - K6 [**4**, 2, **6**, 4], *P1, K5; rep from * to last 7 [**5**, 3, **7**, 5] sts, P1, K6 [**4**, 2, **6**, 4].
Row 5 - Knit.
Row 7 - Inc in first st, K to last st, inc in last st (105 [**113**, 121, **129**, 137] sts).
Row 9 - K4 [**2**, 6, **4**, 2], *P1, K5; rep from * to last 5 [**3**, 7, **5**, 3] sts, P1, K4 [**2**, 6, **4**, 2].
Row 11 - Knit.
Row 12 - Purl.
These 12 rows form patt and set side seam shaping.
Cont in patt, shaping side seams by inc 1 st at each end of every foll 6th row from previous inc until there are 121 [**129**, 137, **145**, 153] sts, taking inc sts into patt.
Work straight until Back meas 26 cm, ending with RS facing for next row.
Shape armholes
Keeping patt correct, cast off 4 [**5**, 6, **7**, 8] sts at beg of next 2 rows
(113 [**119**, 125, **131**, 137] sts).
Next row - (RS), K3, K2tog, patt to last 5 sts, K2tog tbl, K3.
Next row - P3, P2tog tbl, P to last 5 sts, P2tog, P3.
Rep last 2 rows once more
(105 [**111**, 117, **123**, 129] sts).
Next row - (RS), K3, K2tog, patt to last 5 sts, K2tog tbl, K3.
Next row - Purl.
Rep last 2 rows 4 [**5**, 6, **7**, 8] times more
(95 [**99**, 103, **107**, 111] sts).
Work straight until armhole meas 20 [**20**, 21, **21**, 22] cm, ending with RS facing for next row.
Shape shoulders and back neck
Cast off 7 [**7**, 7, **8**, 8] sts at beg of next 4 rows
(67 [**71**, 75, **75**, 79] sts).
Next row - (RS), cast off 7 [**7**, 8, **8**, 8] sts, patt until there are 11 [**12**, 12, **11**, 12] sts on right needle, turn and work this side first.
Cast off 4 sts at beg of next row.
Cast off rem 7 [**8**, 8, **7**, 8] sts.
With RS facing, slip centre 31 [**33**, 35, **37**, 39] sts onto a spare needle, rejoin yarn to rem sts, patt to end. Work to match first side, reversing shapings.

FRONT

Work as Back until 24 rows less have been worked before start of shoulder shaping, thus ending with RS facing for next row.
Shape front neck
Next row - (RS), patt 38 [**39**, 40, **41**, 42], turn and work this side first.
Dec 1 st at neck edge of next 4 rows, then on foll 6 alt rows (28 [**29**, 30, **31**, 32] sts).
Work 7 rows, thus ending with RS facing for next row.
Shape shoulder
Cast off 7 [**7**, 7, **8**, 8] sts at beg of next and foll alt row, then 7 [**8**, 8, **8**, 8] sts at beg of foll alt row.
Work 1 row. Cast off rem 7 [**8**, 8, **7**, 8] sts.
With RS facing, slip centre 19 [**21**, 23, **25**, 27] sts onto a spare needle, rejoin yarn to rem sts, patt to end.
Work to match first side, reversing shapings, working an extra row before start of shoulder shaping.

SLEEVES

With smaller size needles, cast on
81 [**85**, 89, **93**, 97] sts.
Work in rib as on Back for 3 cm, ending with
row 2.

Change to larger size needles and **patt** thus:
Row 1 - (RS), inc in first st, K to last st, inc in
last st (83 [**87**, 91, **95**, 99] sts).
Row 2 and every foll alt row - Purl.
Row 3 - Inc in first st, K1 [**0**, 2, **1**, 0], *P1, K5;
rep from * to last 3 [**2**, 4, **3**, 2] sts, P1, K1 [**0**, 2,
1, 0], inc in last st (85 [**89**, 93, **97**, 101] sts).
Rows 5 and 7 - As row 1
(89 [**93**, 97, **101**, 105] sts).
Row 9 - As row 3 (91 [**95**, 99, **103**, 107] sts).
Row 11 - As row 1 (93 [**97**, 101, **105**, 109] sts).
Row 12 - Purl.
Cont in patt without further shaping until
Sleeve meas 9 cm, ending with RS facing for
next row.

Shape top
Cast off 4 [**5**, 6, **7**, 8] sts at beg of next 2 rows
(85 [**87**, 89, **91**, 93] sts). Working all decreases
3 sts in from ends of rows as set by Back, dec
1 st at each end of next 5 rows, then on every
foll alt row until 27 [**31**, 27, **31**, 27] sts rem,
thus ending with **WS** facing for next row.
Dec 1 st at each end of next 7 [**9**, 7, **9**, 7] rows.
Cast off rem 13 sts.

MAKE UP

Press carefully following instructions on ball
band.
Join right shoulder seam.

Neck Border
With RS facing and smaller size needles, **knit
up** 23 sts down left side of front neck, K 19
[**21**, 23, **25**, 27] sts from Front, **knit up** 23 sts
up right side of front neck, 4 sts down right
side of back neck, K 31 [**33**, 35, **37**, 39] sts
from Back inc 1 st at centre, then **knit up** 4 sts
up left side of back neck
(105 [**109**, 113, **117**, 121] sts).
Starting with rib row 2, work in rib as for Back
for 5 cm. Using a larger size needle, cast off in
rib.
Join left shoulder seam and Neck Border.
Join side seams.
Join sleeve seams.
Insert Sleeves.

CARDIGAN
BACK

With smaller size needles, cast on
109 [**117**, 125, **133**, 141] sts.
Work in rib as on Back of Sweater for 7 cm,
ending with row 2.
Change to larger size needles and **patt** as
given for 1st [**2nd**, 3rd, **4th**, 5th] size of Back of
Sweater, inc 1 st at each end of patt row 7 and
every foll 6th row until there are 127 [**135**, 143,
151, 159] sts, taking inc sts into patt.
Work straight until Back meas 27 cm, ending
with RS facing for next row.

Shape armholes
Keeping patt correct, cast off 4 [**5**, 6, **7**, 8] sts
at beg of next 2 rows
(119 [**125**, 131, **137**, 143] sts).
Next row - (RS), K3, K2tog, patt to last 5 sts,
K2tog tbl, K3.
Next row - P3, P2tog tbl, P to last 5 sts, P2tog,
P3.
Rep last 2 rows once more
(111 [**117**, 123, **129**, 135] sts).
Next row - (RS), K3, K2tog, patt to last 5 sts,
K2tog tbl, K3.
Next row - Purl.
Rep last 2 rows 4 [**5**, 6, **7**, 8] times more
(101 [**105**, 109, **113**, 117] sts).
Work straight until armhole meas 21 [**21**, 22,
22, 23] cm, ending with RS facing for next row.

Shape shoulders and back neck
Cast off 8 sts at beg of next 4 rows
(69 [**73**, 77, **81**, 85] sts).
Next row - (RS), cast off 7 [**8**, 8, **8**, 9] sts, patt
until there are 11 [**11**, 12, **13**, 13] sts on right
needle, turn and work this side first.
Cast off 4 sts at beg of next row.
Cast off rem 7 [**7**, 8, **9**, 9] sts.
With RS facing, rejoin yarn to rem sts, cast off
centre 33 [**35**, 37, **39**, 41] sts, patt to end. Work
to match first side, reversing shapings.

LEFT FRONT

With smaller size needles, cast on 51 [**55**, 59,
63, 67] sts.
Work in rib as on Back of Sweater for 7 cm,
ending with row 2.
Change to larger size needles and **patt** thus:
Row 1 - (RS), Knit.
Row 2 and every foll alt row - Purl.
Row 3 - K6 [**4**, 2, **6**, 4], *P1, K5; rep from * to
last 3 sts, P1, K2.
Row 5 - Knit.
Row 7 - Inc in first st, K to end
(52 [**56**, 60, **64**, 68] sts).
Row 9 - K4 [**2**, 6, **4**, 2], *P1, K5; rep from * to
end.
Row 11 - Knit.
Row 12 - Purl.
These 12 rows form patt and set side seam
shaping.
Cont in patt, shaping side seam by inc 1 st at
beg of every foll 6th row from previous inc until
there are 60 [**64**, 68, **72**, 76] sts, taking inc sts
into patt.
Work straight until Left Front matches Back to
start of armhole shaping, ending with RS
facing for next row.

Shape armhole
Keeping patt correct, cast off 4 [**5**, 6, **7**, 8] sts
at beg of next row (56 [**59**, 62, **65**, 68] sts).
Work 1 row.

Shape front slope
Next row - (RS), K3, K2tog, patt to last 5 sts,
K2tog tbl, K3.
Working all decreases 3 sts in from ends of
rows as set by Back, dec 1 st at armhole edge

of next 3 rows **and at same time** dec 1 st at
front slope edge on 2nd of these rows
(50 [**53**, 56, **59**, 62] sts).

86, 91, 97 and 102 cm sizes: Dec 1 st at each
end of next and foll [**1**, 1, **3**, 4] alt rows
([**49**, 52, **51**, 52] sts).
Work 1 row, thus ending with RS facing for next
row.

All sizes: Dec 1 st at armhole edge of next
and foll 4 [**3**, 4, **3**, 3] alt rows **and at same
time** dec 1 st at front slope edge on every foll
4th row from previous dec
(43 [**43**, 45, **45**, 46] sts).
Dec 1 st at front slope edge **only** on every foll
4th row from previous dec until 30 [**31**, 32, **33**,
34] sts rem.
Work straight until Left Front matches Back to
start of shoulder shaping, ending with RS
facing for next row.

Shape shoulder
Cast off 8 sts at beg of next and foll alt row,
then 7 [**8**, 8, **8**, 9] sts at beg of foll alt row. Work
1 row. Cast off rem 7 [**7**, 8, **9**, 9] sts.

RIGHT FRONT

With smaller size needles, cast on 51 [**55**, 59,
63, 67] sts.
Work in rib as on Back of Sweater for 7 cm,
ending with row 2.
Change to larger size needles and **patt** thus:
Row 1 - (RS), Knit.
Row 2 and every foll alt row - Purl.
Row 3 - K2, *P1, K5; rep from * to last 7 [**5**, 3,
7, 5] sts, P1, K6 [**4**, 2, **6**, 4].
Row 5 - Knit.
Row 7 - K to last st, inc in last st
(52 [**56**, 60, **64**, 68] sts).
Row 9 - *K5, P1; rep from * to last 4 [**2**, 6, **4**, 2]
sts, K4 [**2**, 6, **4**, 2].
Row 11 - Knit.
Row 12 - Purl.
These 12 rows form patt and set side seam
shaping.
Complete to match Left Front, reversing
shapings, working an extra row before start of
armhole and shoulder shaping.

SLEEVES

With smaller size needles, cast on 61 [**63**, 65,
67, 69] sts.
Work in rib as on Back of Sweater for 7 cm,
ending with row 2.
Change to larger size needles and **patt** as
given for 1st [**2nd**, 3rd, **4th**, 5th] size of Back of
Sweater, inc 1 st at each end of patt row 7 and
every foll 6th [**6th**, 6th, **4th**, 4th] row until there
are 91 [**101**, 107, **73**, 81] sts, taking inc sts into
patt.
81, 86, 97 and 102 cm sizes: Inc 1 st at each
end of every foll 8th [**8th**, 6th, 6th] row until
there are 99 [**103**, 111, 115] sts.
All sizes: Work straight until Sleeve meas
46 [**46**, 47, **47**, 47] cm, ending with RS facing
for next row.

Shape top

Keeping patt correct, cast off 4 [**5**, 6, **7**, 8] sts at beg of next 2 rows (91 [**93**, 95, **97**, 99] sts). Working all decreases 3 sts in from ends of rows as set by Back, dec 1 st at each end of next 11 rows, then on every foll alt row until 29 [**33**, 29, **33**, 33] sts rem, thus ending with **WS** facing for next row. Dec 1 st at each end of next 7 [**9**, 7, **9**, 9] rows. Cast off rem 15 sts.

MAKE UP

Press carefully following instructions on ball band.
Join both shoulder seams.

Button Border

With smaller size needles, cast on 7 sts.
Row 1 - (RS), K1, (K1 tbl, P1) twice, K1 tbl, K1.
Row 2 - K1, (P1 tbl, K1) 3 times.
Rep last 2 rows until Border, when slightly stretched, fits up Left Front to start of front slope shaping, up front slope and across to centre back neck, sewing in place as you go along and ending with RS facing for next row. Cast off in rib.
Mark positions for 8 buttons on Button Border with pins to ensure even spacing - first button 1 cm up from lower edge, third button level with top of rib, second button midway between first and third, top button 1 cm below start of front slope shaping and rem 4 buttons evenly spaced between.

Buttonhole Border

Work to match Button Border, with the addition of 8 buttonholes to correspond with positions marked for buttons.
To make a buttonhole (RS): K1, K1 tbl, P1, (yrn) twice (to make a buttonhole - drop extra loop on next row), P2tog, K1 tbl, K1.
Join ends of borders at centre back neck.
Join side seams. Join sleeve seams. Insert Sleeves.
Sew on buttons.

BEADED VERSIONS

Work as for Textured Versions but replace each "P1" of textured patt with "bead 1", worked as follows: bring yarn to front of work and slip bead up next to st just worked, slip next st purlwise from left needle to right needle, take yarn to back of work, leaving bead sitting in front of slipped st.
Before starting, thread required number of beads onto yarn. To do this, thread a fine sewing needle (one that will easily pass through the beads) with sewing thread. Knot ends of thread and then pass end of yarn through this loop. Thread a bead onto the sewing thread and then gently slide it along and onto the knitting yarn. Continue in this way until the required number of beads are on the yarn. Below is a guide to the number of beads required for each section but it is advisable to thread a few more onto yarn as even the best quality glass beads can sometimes break as

they are moved up and down along the yarn.
Sweater: Approx 560 beads for Back, approx 530 beads for Front, and approx 180 beads for each Sleeve.
Cardigan: Approx 600 beads for Back, approx 260 beads for each Front, and approx 490 beads for each Sleeve.

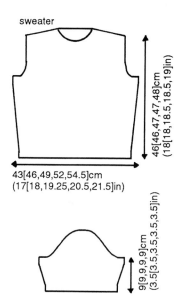

sweater

43[46,49,52,54.5]cm
(17[18,19.25,20.5,21.5]in)

46[46,47,47,48]cm
(18[18,18.5,18.5,19]in)

9[9,9,9]cm
(3.5[3.5,3.5,3.5,3.5]in)

cardigan

45.5[48,51,54,57]cm
(18[19,20,21.25,22.5]in)

48[48,49,49,50]cm
(19[19,19.5,19.5,19.5]in)

46[46,47,47,47]cm
(18[18,18.5,18.5,18.5]in)

Design 2

Heart

To fit bust					
81	**86**	91	**97**	102	cm
32	**34**	36	**38**	40	in
Actual size, at underarm					
91	**96**	102	**108**	114	cm
36	**38**	40	**42½**	45	in
Finished length					
48	**48**	49	**49**	50	cm
19	**19**	19½	**19½**	19½	in
Sleeve length to underarm					
46	**46**	47	**47**	47	cm
18	**18**	18½	**18½**	18½	in

Jaeger Matchmaker Merino 4 ply
(639 and 715)

7	**7**	8	**8**	9	50 gm

Jaeger Cashmere 4 ply

13	**13**	14	**15**	16	25 gm

Jaeger Alpaca 4 ply

7　**7**　8　**8**　9　50 gm

Quantities of yarn are approximate as they are based on average requirements. Check actual yarn colour - as printing may not match yarn exactly.

Matchmaker Merino and Cashmere 4 ply versions: Pair each of 2³/₄ mm (UK 12/USA 2) and 3¹/₄ mm (UK 10/USA 3) needles.
Alpaca 4 ply version: Pair each of 2¹/₄ mm (UK 13/USA 1) and 3 mm (UK 11/USA 2/3) needles.
All versions: 9 buttons.
Beaded version: Approx 1720 [**1760**, 1850, **1940**, 2020] small glass beads.
Ribbon trim version: Approx 1.50 [**1.50**, 1.60, **1.70**, 1.80] metres of narrow satin ribbon.

Tension
28 sts and 36 rows to 10 cm (stocking st) on larger size needles or size needed to achieve stated tension.

For notes and abbreviations, see page 58.

BEADED VERSION

Special note
Beads are attached as garment is knitted. Before starting, thread required number of beads onto yarn. To do this, thread a fine sewing needle (one that will easily pass through the beads) with sewing thread. Knot ends of thread and then pass end of yarn through this loop. Thread a bead onto the sewing thread and then gently slide it along and onto the knitting yarn. Continue in this way until the required number of beads are on the yarn. Pattern specifies number of beads required for each section but it is advisable to thread a few more onto yarn as even the best quality glass beads can sometimes break as they are moved up and down along the yarn.

BACK
Thread approx 390 [**410**, 430, **470**, 490] beads onto yarn.
With smaller size needles, cast on 117 [**123**, 129, **141**, 147] sts.
**Border patt thus:
Row 1 - (RS), Knit.
Row 2 and every foll alt row - Purl.
Rows 3, 5, 7, 9 and 11 - Knit.
Row 13 - K2, *yfwd, K2tog, bring yarn to front of work and slip bead up next to st just worked, slip this st back onto left needle and take yarn to back of work leaving bead on RS, K st just slipped back onto left needle again to secure bead - now termed "eyelet bead 1"; rep from * to last st, K1.
Place markers at both ends of last row.
Row 15 - Knit.
Row 16 - Purl.

Change to larger size needles.
Row 17 - K1, *bring yarn to front of work and slip bead up next to st just worked, slip next st from left needle onto right needle purlwise, take yarn to back of work leaving bead sitting in front of slipped st - now termed "bead 1", K1; rep from * to end.
Row 19 - K1, *K1, bead 1, K3, bead 1; rep from * to last 2 sts, K2.
Row 21 - K1, *bead 1, K5; rep from * to last 2 sts, bead 1, K1.
Row 23 - As row 19.
Row 25 - As row 17.
Row 27 - Knit.
Row 29 - As row 17.
Row 31 - K1, *yfwd, K2tog; rep from * to end.
Row 33 - As row 17.
Row 34 - Purl.
These 34 rows complete border.**
Starting with a K row, work in stocking st for 6 rows.
Next row - (RS), K3, M1 (**by picking up horizontal loop lying before next st and working into back of it**), K to last 3 sts, M1, K3.
Working all increases as set by last row, cont in stocking st, shaping side seams by inc 1 st at each end of every foll 14th [**12th**, 10th, **14th**, 12th] row from previous inc until there are 127 [**135**, 143, **151**, 159] sts.
Work straight until Back meas 28 cm **from markers**, ending with RS facing for next row.
Shape armholes
Cast off 5 [**6**, 7, **8**, 9] sts at beg of next 2 rows (117 [**123**, 129, **135**, 141] sts). Dec 1 st at each end of next 3 [**3**, 3, **5**, 5] rows, then on foll 3 [**5**, 6, **6**, 7] alt rows (105 [**107**, 111, **113**, 117] sts). Work 3 rows, thus ending with RS facing for next row. Dec 1 st at each end of next and every foll 4th row until 99 [**101**, 105, **107**, 111] sts rem.
Work straight until armhole meas 20 [**20**, 21, **21**, 22] cm, ending with RS facing for next row.
Shape shoulders and back neck
Cast off 10 sts at beg of next 2 rows (79 [**81**, 85, **87**, 91] sts).
Next row - (RS), cast off 10 sts, K until there are 13 [**13**, 14, **14**, 15] sts on right needle, turn and work this side first.
Cast off 4 sts at beg of next row.
Cast off rem 9 [**9**, 10, **10**, 11] sts.
With RS facing, rejoin yarn to rem sts, cast off centre 33 [**35**, 37, **39**, 41] sts, K to end. Work to match first side, reversing shapings.

LEFT FRONT
Thread approx 200 [**210**, 220, **240**, 250] beads onto yarn.
With smaller size needles, cast on 60 [**63**, 66, **72**, 75] sts.
Border patt thus:
Row 1 - (RS), Knit.
Row 2 and every foll alt row - Purl.
Rows 3, 5, 7, 9 and 11 - Knit.

Row 13 - K1 [**2**, 1, **1**, 2], *yfwd, K2tog, eyelet bead 1; rep from * to last st, K1.
Place markers at both ends of last row.
Row 15 - Knit.
Row 16 - Purl.
Change to larger size needles.
Row 17 - K1, *bead 1, K1; rep from * to last 1 [**0**, 1, **1**, 0] st, K1 [**0**, 1, **1**, 0].
Row 19 - K1, *K1, bead 1, K3, bead 1; rep from * to last 5 [**2**, 5, **5**, 2] sts, (K1, bead 1) 1 [**0**, 1, **1**, 0] time, K3 [**2**, 3, **3**, 2].
Row 21 - K1, *bead 1, K5; rep from * to last 5 [**2**, 5, **5**, 2] sts, bead 1, K4 [**1**, 4, **4**, 1].
Row 23 - As row 19.
Row 25 - As row 17.
Row 27 - Knit.
Row 29 - As row 17.
Row 31 - K1, *yfwd, K2tog; rep from * to last 1 [**0**, 1, **1**, 0] st, K1 [**0**, 1, **1**, 0].
Row 33 - As row 17.
Row 34 - Purl.
These 34 rows complete border.
Starting with a K row, work in stocking st for 6 rows.
Working all increases as set by Back, cont in stocking st, shaping side seams by inc 1 st at beg of next and every foll 14th [**12th**, 10th, **14th**, 12th] row until there are 65 [**69**, 73, **77**, 81] sts.
Work straight until Left Front matches Back to start of armhole shaping, ending with RS facing for next row.
Shape armhole
Cast off 5 [**6**, 7, **8**, 9] sts at beg of next row (60 [**63**, 66, **69**, 72] sts). Work 1 row. Dec 1 st at armhole edge of next 3 [**3**, 3, **5**, 5] rows, then on foll 3 [**5**, 6, **6**, 7] alt rows (54 [**55**, 57, **58**, 60] sts). Work 3 rows, thus ending with RS facing for next row. Dec 1 st at armhole edge next and every foll 4th row until 51 [**52**, 54, **55**, 57] sts rem.
Cont straight until 23 rows less have been worked than on Back to start of shoulder shaping, ending with **WS** facing for next row.
Shape neck
Cast off 9 [**10**, 11, **12**, 13] sts at beg of next row, and 4 sts at beg of foll alt row (38 [**38**, 39, **39**, 40] sts). Dec 1 st at neck edge of next 4 rows, then on foll 3 alt rows (31 [**31**, 32, **32**, 33] sts). Work 3 rows. Dec 1 st at neck edge of next and foll 4th row (29 [**29**, 30, **30**, 31] sts). Work 2 rows, end with RS facing for next row.
Shape shoulder
Cast off 10 sts at beg of next and foll alt row. Work 1 row. Cast off rem 9 [**9**, 10, **10**, 11] sts.

RIGHT FRONT
Thread approx 200 [**210**, 220, **240**, 250] beads onto yarn.
With smaller size needles, cast on 60 [**63**, 66, **72**, 75] sts.
Border patt thus:
Row 1 - (RS), Knit.
Row 2 and every foll alt row - Purl.

Rows 3, 5, 7, 9 and 11 - Knit.
Row 13 - K1, *yfwd, K2tog, eyelet bead 1; rep from * to last 1 [**2**, 1, **1**, 2] sts, K1 [**2**, 1, **1**, 2]. Place markers at both ends of last row.
Row 15 - Knit.
Row 16 - Purl.
Change to larger size needles.
Row 17 - K2 [**1**, 2, **2**, 1], *bead 1, K1; rep from * to end.
Row 19 - K3 [**2**, 3, **3**, 2], (bead 1, K1) 1 [**0**, 1, **1**, 0] time, *bead 1, K3, bead 1, K1; rep from * to last st, K1.
Row 21 - K4 [**1**, 4, **4**, 1], *bead 1, K5; rep from * to last 2 sts, bead 1, K1.
Row 23 - As row 19.
Row 25 - As row 17.
Row 27 - Knit.
Row 29 - As row 17.
Row 31 - K2 [**1**, 2, **2**, 1], *yfwd, K2tog; rep from * to end.
Row 33 - As row 17.
Row 34 - Purl.
These 34 rows complete border.
Complete to match Left Front, reversing shapings, working an extra row before start of armhole, neck and shoulder shaping.

SLEEVES

Thread approx 210 [**210**, 230, **230**, 250] beads onto yarn.
With smaller size needles, cast on 63 [**63**, 69, **69**, 75] sts.
Work Border as on Back from ** to **.
Starting with a K row and working all increases in same way as those up side seams, work in stocking st, shaping sides by inc 1 st at each end of 9th [**9th**, 9th, **7th**, 9th] row and every foll 8th row until there are 73 [**93**, 85, **103**, 101] sts.
81, 86, 91 and 102 cm sizes: Inc 1 st at each end of every foll 10th row until there are 91 [**95**, 99, **107**] sts.
All sizes: Work straight until Sleeve meas 46 [**46**, 47, **47**, 47] cm **from markers**, ending with RS facing for next row.
Shape top
Cast off 5 [**6**, 7, **8**, 9] sts at beg of next 2 rows (81 [**83**, 85, **87**, 89] sts). Dec 1 st at each end of next 5 rows, then on every foll alt row until 67 sts rem. Work 3 rows, thus ending with RS facing for next row. Dec 1 st at each end of next and every foll 4th row until 57 sts rem, then on foll 5 [**3**, 5, **3**, 5] alt rows, thus ending with **WS** facing for next row (47 [**51**, 47, **51**, 47] sts). Dec 1 st at each end of next 5 [**7**, 5, **7**, 5] rows (37 sts).
Cast off 4 sts at beg of next 4 rows.
Cast off rem 21 sts.

MAKE UP

Press carefully following instructions on ball band.
Join shoulder and side seams. Fold lower edge to inside along first (beaded) eyelet row and loosely stitch in place.

Front Borders (Both alike)
Thread approx 170 beads onto yarn.
With RS facing and smaller size needles, **knit up** 109 [**109**, 111, **111**, 113] sts along front opening edge between neck shaping and folded lower edge.
***Row 1 and every foll alt row** - (WS), Purl.
Row 2 - K1, *bead 1, K1; rep from * to end.
Row 4 - K1, *yfwd, K2tog; rep from * to end.
Row 6 - As row 2.
Row 8 - K1, *yfwd, K2tog, eyelet bead 1; rep from * to last 2 sts, yfwd, K2tog.
Row 10 - Knit.
Row 12 - As row 4.
Row 14 - Knit.
Row 15 - Purl.
Cast off.
Fold Border in half to inside along second (beaded) eyelet row and loosely stitch in place.***
Work Border along other front opening edge in same way.
Neck Border
Thread approx 170 [**170**, 180, **190**, 190] beads onto yarn.
With RS facing and smaller size needles, **knit up** 5 sts across top of right front Border, 31 [**32**, 33, **34**, 35] sts up right side of neck, 37 [**39**, 41, **43**, 45] sts across back neck, 31 [**32**, 33, **34**, 35] sts down left side of neck, then 5 sts across top of left front Border (109 [**113**, 117, **121**, 125] sts).
Work as for Front Borders from *** to ***.
Join sleeve seams. Fold lower edge to inside along first (beaded) eyelet row and loosely stitch in place. Insert Sleeves.
Using eyelet holes of borders as buttonholes, sew on buttons, positioning lowest button 1.5 cm up from lower edge, top button level with eyelet row in Neck Border and rem 7 buttons evenly spaced between.

RIBBON TRIM VERSION

Work as for Beaded Version but do not thread beads onto yarn, omit "eyelet bead 1" from all relevant rows and replace "bead 1" with "P1" throughout.
Thread ribbon in and out of uppermost eyelet row around lower edge of body and sleeves.

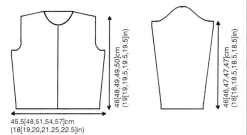

45.5[48,51,54,57]cm
(18[19,20,21.25,22.5]in)

48[48,49,49,50]cm
(19[19,19.5,19.5,19.5]in)

46[46,47,47,47]cm
(18[18,18.5,18.5,18.5]in)

To fit bust/chest							
81	**86**	91	**97**	102	**107**	112	cm
32	**34**	36	**38**	40	**42**	44	in
Actual size							
107	**111**	117	**121**	127	**131**	137	cm
42	**43½**	46	**47½**	50	**51½**	54	in
Finished length							
69	**69**	70	**70**	71	**71**	72	cm
27	**27**	27½	**27½**	28	**28**	28½	in
Sleeve length to underarm							
46	**46**	48	**50**	50	**52**	52	cm
18	**18**	19	**19½**	19½	**20½**	20½	in

Jaeger Matchmaker Merino 4 ply
Crew neck version (718)

10	**10**	11	**11**	12	**12**	13	50 gm

Polo neck version

10	**10**	11	**12**	12	**13**	13	50 gm

Jaeger Cashmere 4 Ply
Crew neck version

| 16 | **16** | 17 | **18** | 19 | **20** | 21 | 25 gm |

Polo neck version (108)

| 17 | **17** | 18 | **19** | 20 | **21** | 22 | 25 gm |

Jaeger Alpaca 4 Ply
Crew neck version

| 10 | **10** | 11 | **11** | 12 | **12** | 13 | 50 gm |

Polo neck version

| 10 | **10** | 11 | **12** | 12 | **13** | 13 | 50 gm |

Quantities of yarn are approximate as they are based on average requirements.

Check actual yarn colour - as printing may not match yarn exactly.

Matchmaker Merino and Cashmere 4 ply versions: Pair each of 2³/₄ mm (UK 12/USA 2) and 3¹/₄ mm (UK 10/USA 3) needles.
Alpaca 4 ply versions: Pair each of 2¹/₄ mm (UK 13/USA 1) and 3 mm (UK 11/USA 2/3) needles.

Tension
28 sts and 36 rows to 10 cm (stocking st) on larger size needles or size needed to achieve stated tension.
It is important to check your tension before starting your garment. If there are too many stitches to 10 cm, your tension is tight and you should change to a larger size needle. If there are too few, your tension is loose and you should change to a smaller size needle.

For notes and abbreviations, see page 58.

BACK
With smaller size needles, cast on 150 [**154**, 162, **170**, 178, **182**, 190] sts.
Rib row 1 - (RS), (K1 tbl) twice, *(P1 tbl) twice, (K1 tbl) twice; rep from * to end.
Rib row 2 - (P1 tbl) twice, *(K1 tbl) twice, (P1 tbl) twice; rep from * to end.
81, 97 and 102 cm sizes only: Rep these 2 rows for 15 cm for ladies version or 10 cm for mans version, ending with row 2.
86, 91, 107 and 112 cm sizes only: Rep these 2 rows for 15 cm for ladies version or 10 cm for mans version, inc 1 st at each end of last row and ending with row 2
([**156**, 164, **184**, 192] sts).
All sizes: Change to larger size needles and starting with a K row, work in stocking st until Back meas 46 cm, ending with RS facing for next row.
Shape armholes
Cast off 6 sts at beg of next 2 rows
(138 [**144**, 152, **158**, 166, **172**, 180] sts).
Next row - (RS), K3, K2tog, K to last 5 sts, K2tog tbl, K3.
Next row - Purl.
Rep last 2 rows 9 times more
(118 [**124**, 132, **138**, 146, **152**, 160] sts).

Cont straight until armholes meas 23 [**23**, 24, **24**, 25, **25**, 26] cm, ending with RS facing for next row.
Shape shoulders and back neck
Cast off 10 [**10**, 11, **12**, 12, **13**, 14] sts at beg of next 4 rows
(78 [**84**, 88, **90**, 98, **100**, 104] sts).
Next row - (RS), cast off 9 [**10**, 11, **11**, 12, **13**, 14] sts, K until there are 13 [**14**, 15, **15**, 17, **17**, 17] sts on right needle, turn and work this side first.
Cast off 4 sts at beg of next row.
Cast off rem 9 [**10**, 11, **11**, 13, **13**, 13] sts.
With RS facing, slip centre 34 [**36**, 36, **38**, 40, **40**, 42] sts on a spare needle, rejoin yarn to rem sts, K to end.
Work to match first side, reversing shapings.

FRONT
Work as Back until 24 [**26**, 26, **28**, 28, **30**, 30] rows less have been worked before start of shoulder shaping, thus ending with RS facing for next row.
Shape neck
Next row - (RS), K49 [**51**, 55, **58**, 61, **64**, 68] sts, turn and work this side first.
Dec 1 st at neck edge on next 6 rows, then on every foll alt row until 38 [**40**, 44, **46**, 49, **52**, 55] sts rem.
Work 7 [**9**, 9, **9**, 9, **11**, 9] rows, thus ending with RS facing for next row.
Shape shoulder
Cast off 10 [**10**, 11, **12**, 12, **13**, 14] sts at beg of next and foll alt row, then 9 [**10**, 11, **11**, 12, **13**, 14] sts at beg of foll alt row.
Work 1 row.
Cast off rem 9 [**10**, 11, **11**, 13, **13**, 13] sts.
With RS facing, slip centre 20 [**22**, 22, **22**, 24, **24**, 24] sts on a spare needle, rejoin yarn to rem sts, K to end.
Work to match first side, reversing shapings, working an extra row before start of shoulder shaping.

SLEEVES
With smaller size needles, cast on 70 [**70**, 74, **78**, 82, **82**, 82] sts.
Work in rib as for Back for 6 cm, ending with row 2.
Change to larger size needles and, starting with a K row, work in stocking st, shaping sides by inc 1 st at each end of 5th and every foll 4th row to 118 [**118**, 120, **106**, 116, **108**, 126] sts, then on every foll 6th row (from previous inc) until there are 128 [**128**, 134, **134**, 140, **140**, 146] sts.
Cont straight until Sleeve meas 46 [**46**, 48, **50**, 50, **52**, 52] cm, ending with RS facing for next row.
Shape top
Cast off 6 sts at beg of next 2 rows
(116 [**116**, 122, **122**, 128, **128**, 134] sts).
Next row - (RS), K3, K2tog, K to last 5 sts, K2tog tbl, K3.

Next row - Purl.
Rep last 2 rows 9 times more.
Cast off rem 96 [**96**, 102, **102**, 108, **108**, 114] sts.

MAKE UP
Press carefully following instructions on ball band.
Join right shoulder seam.
Neck Border
With RS facing and smaller size needles, **knit up** 24 [**26**, 26, **27**, 27, **29**, 30] sts down left side of front neck, K 20 [**22**, 22, **22**, 24, **24**, 24] from Front, **knit up** 24 [**26**, 26, **27**, 27, **29**, 30] sts up right side of front neck, 4 sts down right side of back neck, K 34 [**36**, 36, **38**, 40, **40**, 42] from Back, then **knit up** 4 sts up left side of back neck (110 [**118**, 118, **122**, 126, **130**, 134] sts).
Starting with rib row 2, work in rib as for Back for 3 cm.
Crew neck version only: Using larger size needle, cast off in rib.
Join left shoulder seam and Neck Border.
Polo neck version only: Change to larger size needles and cont in rib until Neck Border meas 16 cm. Cast off **loosely** in rib.
Join left shoulder seam and Neck Border, reversing seam for turn-back.
Both versions: Place centre of cast-off edge of Sleeves to shoulder seams and sew Sleeves to Back and Front, matching shaped edges.
Join side and sleeve seams.

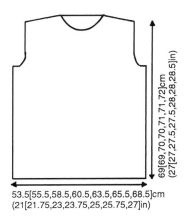

69[69,70,70,71,71,72]cm
(27[27,27.5,27.5,28,28,28.5]in)

53.5[55.5,58.5,60.5,63.5,65.5,68.5]cm
(21[21.75,23,23.75,25,25.75,27]in)

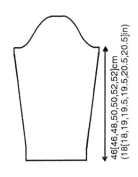

46[46,48,50,50,52,52]cm
(18[18,19,19.5,19.5,20.5,20.5]in)

Design 4

Drift

To fit bust

81	**86**	91	**97**	102	cm
32	**34**	36	**38**	40	in

Actual size

107	**113**	119	**125**	131	cm
42	**44½**	47	**49**	51½	in

Finished length

66	**66**	67	**67**	68	cm
26	**26**	26½	**26½**	27	in

Sleeve length to underarm

46	**46**	47	**47**	47	cm
18	**18**	18½	**18½**	18½	in

Jaeger Matchmaker Merino 4 ply

10	**10**	10	**11**	11	50 gm

Jaeger Cashmere 4 ply

17	**18**	19	**20**	21	25 gm

Jaeger Alpaca 4 ply (148)

10	**10**	10	**11**	11	50 gm

Quantities of yarn are approximate as they are based on average requirements. Check actual yarn colour - as printing may not match yarn exactly.

Matchmaker Merino and Cashmere 4 ply versions: Pair each of 2¾ mm (UK 12/USA 2) and 3¼ mm (UK 10/USA 3) needles.
2¾ mm (UK 12/USA 2) circular needle.
Alpaca 4 ply version: Pair each of 2¼ mm (UK 13/USA 1) and 3 mm (UK 11/USA 2/3) needles.
2¼ mm (UK 13/USA 1) circular needle.
All versions: Cable pin.

Tension
30 sts and 36 rows to 10 cm (patt), 28 sts and 36 rows to 10 cm (stocking st) on larger size needles or size needed to achieve stated tension.

For notes and abbreviations, see page 58.

Special abbreviations
C3F=slip next 2 sts on cable pin and leave at front of work, K1 tbl, slip 2nd st from cable pin back onto left needle and P this st, then K1 tbl from cable pin.

BACK

With smaller size needles, cast on 142 [**150**, 158, **166**, 174] sts.
Rib row 1 - (RS), P2, *(K1 tbl) twice, P2; rep from * to end.
Rib row 2 - K2, *(P1 tbl) twice, K2; rep from * to end.
Rep these 2 rows for 7 cm, ending with **WS** facing for next row.
Increase row - (**WS**), *K2, P1 tbl, M1 (**by picking up horizontal loop lying before next st and working into back of it**), P1 tbl, K2, (P1 tbl) twice; rep from * to last 6 sts, K2, P1 tbl, M1, P1 tbl, K2 (160 [**169**, 178, **187**, 196] sts).
Change to larger size needles and **patt** thus:
Row 1 - (RS), *P2, K1 tbl, P1, K1 tbl, P2, (K1 tbl) twice; rep from * to last 7 sts, P2, K1 tbl, P1, K1 tbl, P2.
Row 2 and every foll alt row - *K2, P1 tbl, K1, P1 tbl, K2, (P1 tbl) twice; rep from * to last 7 sts, K2, P1 tbl, K1, P1 tbl, K2.
Row 3 - *P2, C3F, P2, (K1 tbl) twice; rep from * to last 7 sts, P2, C3F, P2.
Row 5 - As row 1.
Row 6 - As row 2.
These 6 rows form patt.
Cont in patt until Back meas 43 cm, ending with RS facing for next row.
Shape armholes
Keeping patt correct, cast off 8 sts at beg of next 2 rows (144 [**153**, 162, **171**, 180] sts).
Dec 1 st at each end of next and foll 9 alt rows (124 [**133**, 142, **151**, 160] sts).
Work straight until armhole meas 23 [**23**, 24, **24**, 25] cm, ending with RS facing for next row.
Shape shoulders and back neck
Keeping patt correct, cast off 13 [**14**, 15, **17**, 18] sts at beg of next 2 rows
(98 [**105**, 112, **117**, 124] sts).
Next row - (RS), cast off 13 [**14**, 15, **17**, 18] sts, patt until there are 16 [**18**, 20, **20**, 22] sts on right needle, turn and work this side first.
Cast off 4 sts at beg of next row.
Cast off rem 12 [**14**, 16, **16**, 18] sts.
With RS facing, rejoin yarn to rem sts, cast off centre 40 [**41**, 42, **43**, 44] sts, patt to end.
Work to match first side, reversing shapings.

FRONT

Work as Back until 22 rows less have been worked before start of shoulder and back neck shaping, thus ending with RS facing for next row.
Shape front neck
Next row - (RS), patt 50 [**54**, 58, **62**, 66], turn and work this side first.
Keeping patt correct, cast off 4 sts at beg of next row
(46 [**50**, 54, **58**, 62] sts).
Dec 1 st at neck edge on next 4 rows, then on foll 2 alt rows
(40 [**44**, 48, **52**, 56] sts).
Work 3 rows.
Dec 1 st at neck edge of next and foll 4th row
(38 [**42**, 46, **50**, 54] sts).
Work 4 rows, thus ending with RS facing for next row.
Shape shoulder
Cast off 13 [**14**, 15, **17**, 18] sts at beg of next and foll alt row. Work 1 row.
Cast off rem 12 [**14**, 16, **16**, 18] sts.
With RS facing, slip centre 24 [**25**, 26, **27**, 28] sts onto a spare needle, rejoin yarn to rem sts, patt to end. Work to match first side, reversing shapings, working an extra row before start of shoulder shaping.

SLEEVES

With smaller size needles, cast on 70 sts.
Work in rib as on Back for 7 cm, ending with **WS** facing for next row
Increase row - (**WS**), *K2, P1 tbl, M1, P1 tbl, K2, (P1 tbl) twice; rep from * to last 6 sts, K2, P1 tbl, M1, P1 tbl, K2 (79 sts).
Change to larger size needles and **patt** thus:
Row 1 - (RS), inc in first st, P1, *K1 tbl, P1, K1 tbl, P2, (K1 tbl) twice, P2; rep from * to last 5 sts, K1 tbl, P1, K1 tbl, P1, inc in last st
(81 sts).
Row 2 - P1 tbl, K2, *P1 tbl, K1, P1 tbl, K2, (P1 tbl) twice, K2; rep from * to last 6 sts, P1 tbl, K1, P1 tbl, K2, P1 tbl.
Row 3 - (Inc in first st) 0 [**0**, 1, **1**, 1] time, (K1 tbl) 1 [**1**, 0, **0**, 0] time, P2, *C3F, P2, (K1 tbl) twice, P2; rep from * to last 6 sts, C3F, P2, (K1 tbl) 1 [**1**, 0, **0**, 0] time, (inc in last st) 0 [**0**, 1, **1**, 1] time
(81 [**81**, 83, **83**, 83] sts).
Row 4 - (P1 tbl) 1 [**1**, 2, **2**, 2] times, K2, *P1 tbl, K1, P1 tbl, K2, (P1 tbl) twice, K2; rep from * to last 6 [**6**, 7, **7**, 7] sts, P1 tbl, K1, P1 tbl, K2, (P1 tbl) 1 [**1**, 2, **2**, 2] times.
Row 5 - (Inc in first st), 1 [**1**, 0, **0**, 1] time, (K1 tbl) 0 [**0**, 2, **2**, 1] times, P2, *K1 tbl, P1, K1 tbl, P2, (K1 tbl) twice, P2; rep from * to last 6 [**6**, 7, **7**, 7] sts, K1 tbl, P1, K1 tbl, P2, (K1 tbl) 0 [**0**, 2, **2**, 1] times, (inc in last st) 1 [**1**, 0, **0**, 1] time
(83 [**83**, 83, **83**, 85] sts).
Row 6 - K0 [**0**, 0, **0**, 1], (P1 tbl) twice, K2, *P1 tbl, K1, P1 tbl, K2, (P1 tbl) twice, K2; rep from * to last 7 [**7**, 7, **7**, 8] sts, P1 tbl, K1, P1 tbl, K2, (P1 tbl) twice, K0 [**0**, 0, **0**, 1].
These 6 rows form patt.
Cont in patt, shaping sides by inc 1 st at each end of every foll 4th [**4th**, 4th, **4th**, alt] row **from previous inc** until there are 133 [**133**, 145, **145**, 95] sts, taking inc sts into patt.
81, 86 and 102 cm sizes: Inc 1 st at each end of every foll 6th [**6th**, 4th] row until there are 139 [**139**, 151] sts.

All sizes: Work straight until Sleeve meas 46 [**46**, 47, **47**, 47] cm, ending with RS facing for next row.

Shape top
Keeping patt correct, cast off 8 sts at beg of next 2 rows (123 [**123**, 129, **129**, 135] sts).
Dec 1 st at each end of next and foll 8 alt rows, thus ending with **WS** facing for next row (105 [**105**, 111, **111**, 117] sts).
Dec 1 st at each end of next row.
Cast off rem 103 [**103**, 109, **109**, 115] sts in patt.

MAKE UP
Press carefully following instructions on ball band.
Join both shoulder seams.

Neck Border
With RS facing and circular needle, starting at left shoulder seam, **knit up** 25 sts down left side of front neck, K 24 [**25**, 26, **27**, 28] sts from front inc 0 [**1**, 0, **1**, 0] st at centre, **knit up** 25 sts up right side of front neck, then 46 [**48**, 48, **50**, 50] sts across back neck (120 [**124**, 124, **128**, 128] sts).
Working in **rounds**, proceed thus:
Next round - (RS), P0 [**1**, 1, **2**, 2], *(K1 tbl) twice, P2; rep from * to last 4 [**3**, 3, **2**, 2] sts, (K1 tbl) twice, P2 [**1**, 1, **0**, 0].
Rep last round 8 times more.

Divide for collar
Next round - (RS), rib 37 [**38**, 38, **39**, 39] and turn.
Now working backwards and forwards in **rows**, not rounds, proceed thus:
Row 1 - (RS of collar, WS of garment), K1, *(K1 tbl) twice, P2; rep from * to last 3 sts, (K1 tbl) twice, K1.
Row 2 - K1, *(P1 tbl) twice, K2; rep from * to last 3 sts, (P1 tbl) twice, K1.
Rep last 2 rows until Collar meas 8 cm from divide. Cast off loosely in rib.
Place centre of cast-off edge of Sleeves to shoulder seams, then sew Sleeves into armholes, matching shaped edges. Join side and sleeve seams.

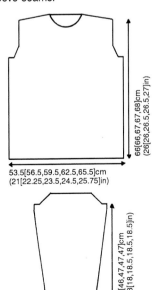

66[66,66,67,68]cm
(26[26,26.5,26.5,27]in)

53.5[56.5,59.5,62.5,65.5]cm
(21[22.25,23.5,24.5,25.75]in)

46[46,47,47,47]cm
(18[18,18.5,18.5,18.5]in)

Design 5

Peace

To fit chest/bust											
61	**66**	71	**76**	81	**86**	91	**97**	102	**107**	112	cm
24	**26**	28	**30**	32	**34**	36	**38**	40	**42**	44	in
Actual size											
75	**82**	89	**96**	104	**111**	118	**125**	133	**140**	147	cm
29¹/₂	**32¹/₂**	35	**38**	41	**43¹/₂**	46¹/₂	**49**	52¹/₂	**55**	58	in
Finished length											
Short version											
41	**45**	49	**52**	54	**56**	57	**57**	58	**58**	59	cm
16	**17¹/₂**	19¹/₂	**20¹/₂**	21¹/₂	**22**	22¹/₂	**22¹/₂**	23	**23**	23	in
Long version											
51	**56**	61	**65**	68	**71**	72	**72**	73	**73**	74	cm
20	**22**	24	**25¹/₂**	27	**28**	28¹/₂	**28¹/₂**	28¹/₂	**28¹/₂**	29	in
Sleeve length to underarm											
33	**36**	39	**42**	44	**46**	47	**48**	49	**50**	50	cm
13	**14**	15¹/₂	**16¹/₂**	17¹/₂	**18**	18¹/₂	**19**	19¹/₂	**19¹/₂**	19¹/₂	in
Jaeger Matchmaker Merino DK											
Short version (864 and 857)											
6	**6**	7	**8**	9	**10**	11	**11**	12	**12**	13	50 gm
Long version (783)											
8	**9**	10	**11**	13	**14**	15	**15**	17	**18**	18	50 gm
Jaeger Extra Fine Merino DK											
Short version											
6	**6**	7	**8**	9	**10**	11	**11**	12	**12**	13	50 gm
Long version (931)											
8	**9**	10	**11**	13	**14**	15	**15**	17	**17**	18	50 gm

Quantities of yarn are approximate as they are based on average requirements.
Check actual yarn colour - as printing may not match yarn exactly.

Matchmaker Merino DK versions: Pair each of 3¹/₄ mm (UK 10/USA 3) and 4 mm (UK 8/USA 6) needles.
Extra Fine Merino DK versions: Pair each of 3 mm (UK 11/USA 2/3) and 3³/₄ mm (UK 9/USA 5) needles.

Tension
Matchmaker Merino DK versions: 22 sts and 30 rows to 10 cm (stocking st) on 4 mm (USA 6) needles or size needed to achieve stated tension.
Extra Fine Merino DK versions: 22 sts and 32 rows to 10 cm (stocking st) on 3³/₄ mm (USA 5) needles or size needed to achieve stated tension.

For notes and abbreviations, see page 58.

BACK

With smaller size needles, cast on 82 [**90**, 98, **106**, 114, **122**, 130, **138**, 146, **154**, 162] sts.

Rib row 1 - (RS), K2, *P2, K2; rep from * to end.

Rib row 2 - P2, *K2, P2; rep from * to end.
Rep last 2 rows for 6 [**6**, 6, **6**, 8, **8**, 8, **8**, 8, **8**, 8] cm, ending with RS facing for next row.

Change to larger size needles.

Short version only: Starting with a K row, work in stocking st until Back meas 23 [**26**, 29, **31**, 32, **33**, 33, **33**, 33, **33**, 33] cm, ending with RS facing for next row.

Long version only: Starting with a K row, work in stocking st until Back meas 33 [**37**, 41, **44**, 46, **48**, 48, **48**, 48, **48**, 48] cm, ending with RS facing for next row.

All versions:

Shape armholes

Cast off 5 [**5**, 5, **5**, 6, **6**, 6, **6**, 6, **6**, 6] sts at beg of next 2 rows
(72 [**80**, 88, **96**, 102, **110**, 118, **126**, 134, **142**, 150] sts).
Work straight until armhole meas 18 [**19**, 20, **21**, 22, **23**, 24, **24**, 25, **25**, 26] cm, ending with RS facing for next row.

Shape shoulders and back neck

Cast off 7 [**8**, 9, **10**, 11, **12**, 14, **15**, 16, **17**, 18] sts at beg of next 2 rows (58 [**64**, 70, **76**, 80, **86**, 90, **96**, 102, **108**, 114] sts).

Next row - (RS), cast off 7 [**8**, 9, **10**, 11, **12**, 14, **15**, 16, **17**, 18] sts, K until there are 11 [**13**, 14, **15**, 16, **17**, 17, **18**, 19, **21**, 22] sts on right needle, turn and work this side first.
Cast off 4 sts at beg of next row.
Cast off rem 7 [**9**, 10, **11**, 12, **13**, 13, **14**, 15, **17**, 18] sts.
With RS facing, slip centre 22 [**22**, 24, **26**, 26, **28**, 28, **30**, 32, **32**, 34] sts onto a spare needle, rejoin yarn to rem sts, K to end. Work to match first side, reversing shapings.

FRONT

Work as Back until 14 [**14**, 16, **16**, 16, **18**, 18, **18**, 18, **20**, 20] rows less have been worked before start of shoulder and back neck shaping, thus ending with RS facing for next row.

Shape front neck

Next row - (RS), K30 [**34**, 37, **40**, 44, **47**, 51, **54**, 59, **63**, 66], turn and work this side first.
Cast off 4 sts at beg of next row
(26 [**30**, 33, **36**, 40, **43**, 47, **50**, 55, **59**, 62] sts).
Dec 1 st at neck edge on next 2 [**2**, 2, **2**, 4, **4**, 4, **4**, 4, **4**, 4] rows, then on foll 3 [**3**, 3, **3**, 2, **2**, 2, **2**, 4, **4**, 4] alt rows
(21 [**25**, 28, **31**, 34, **37**, 41, **44**, 47, **51**, 54] sts).
Work 4 [**4**, 6, **6**, 6, **8**, 8, **8**, 4, **6**, 6] rows, thus ending with RS facing for next row.

Shape shoulder

Cast off 7 [**8**, 9, **10**, 11, **12**, 14, **15**, 16, **17**, 18] sts at beg of next and foll alt row.
Work 1 row.
Cast off rem 7 [**9**, 10, **11**, 12, **13**, 13, **14**, 15, **17**, 18] sts.
With RS facing, slip centre 12 [**12**, 14, **16**, 14, **16**, 16, **18**, 16, **16**, 18] sts onto a spare needle, rejoin yarn to rem sts, K to end.
Work to match first side, reversing shapings, working an extra row before start of shoulder shaping.

SLEEVES

With smaller size needles, cast on 46 [**46**, 50, **54**, 54, **58**, 58, **58**, 62, **62**, 62] sts.
Work in rib as on Back for 6 [**6**, 6, **6**, 8, **8**, 8, **8**, 8, **8**, 8] cm, ending with RS facing for next row.

Change to larger size needles and starting with a K row, work in stocking st, shaping sides by inc 1 st at each end of next and every foll 4th row to 74 [**78**, 72, **68**, 80, **84**, 92, **90**, 90, **88**, 100] sts, then on every foll 6th row until there are 80 [**84**, 88, **92**, 96, **102**, 106, **106**, 110, **110**, 114] sts.
Work straight until Sleeve meas 33 [**36**, 39, **42**, 44, **46**, 47, **48**, 49, **50**, 50] cm, ending with RS facing for next row.

Shape top

Place markers at both ends of last row to denote top of sleeve seam.
Work a further 6 [**6**, 6, **6**, 8, **8**, 8, **8**, 8, **8**, 8] rows, thus ending with RS facing for next row.
Cast off loosely.

MAKE UP

Press carefully following instructions on ball band.
Join right shoulder seam.

Neck Border

With RS facing and smaller size needles, **knit up** 18 [**18**, 20, **20**, 21, **23**, 23, **23**, 25, **27**, 27] sts down left side of front neck, K 12 [**12**, 14, **16**, 14, **16**, 16, **18**, 16, **16**, 18] sts from front, **knit up** 18 [**18**, 20, **20**, 21, **23**, 23, **23**, 25, **27**, 27] sts up right side of front neck, 4 sts down right side of back neck, K 22 [**22**, 24, **26**, 26, **28**, 28, **30**, 32, **32**, 34] sts from back, then **knit up** 4 sts up left side of back neck
(78 [**78**, 86, **90**, 90, **98**, 98, **102**, 106, **110**, 114] sts).

Crew neck version: Starting with row 2, work in rib as on Back for 3 cm.

Turtle neck version: Starting with row 2, work in rib as on Back for 6 [**6**, 6, **6**, 8, **8**, 8, **8**, 8, **8**, 8] cm.

Polo neck version: Starting with row 2, work in rib as on Back for 4 [**4**, 4, **4**, 5, **5**, 5, **5**, 6, **6**, 6] cm.

Change to larger size needles and cont in rib until Neck Border meas 14 [**14**, 14, **14**, 16, **16**, 16, **16**, 18, **18**, 18] cm.

All versions: Cast off loosely in rib.
Join left shoulder seam and Neck Border, reversing Neck Border seam for last 9 [**9**, 9, **9**, 10, **10**, 10, **10**, 11, **11**, 11] cm for Polo neck version.

Place centre of cast-off edge of Sleeves to shoulder seams, then sew Sleeves into armholes, matching sleeve markers to top of side seams.
Join side and sleeve seams.

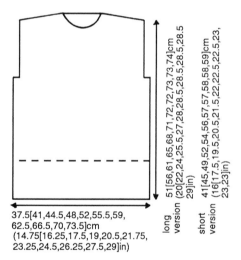

37.5[41,44.5,48,52,55.5,59,
62.5,66.5,70,73.5]cm
(14.75[16.25,17.5,19,20.5,21.75,
23.25,24.5,26.25,27.5,29]in)

long version 51[56,61,65,68,71,72,72,73,73,74]cm (20[22,24,25.5,27,28,28.5,28.5,28.5,28.5,29]in)

short version 41[45,49,52,54,56,57,58,58,59]cm (16[17.5,19.5,20.5,21.5,22,22.5,23,23,23]in)

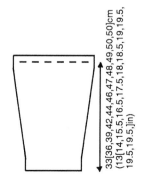

33[36,39,42,44,46,47,48,49,50]cm
(13[14,15.5,16.5,17.5,18,18.5,19,19.5,
19.5,19.5]in)

Design 6

Calm

To fit bust

81	**86**	91	**97**	102	cm
32	**34**	36	**38**	40	in

Actual size
Tunic

100	**105**	111	**116**	122	cm
39¹/₂	**41¹/₂**	43¹/₂	**45¹/₂**	48	in

Jacket

109	**115**	120	**125**	131	cm
43	**45¹/₂**	47	**49**	51¹/₂	in

Finished length
Tunic

66	**66**	67	**67**	68	cm
26	**26**	26¹/₂	**26¹/₂**	27	in

Jacket

71	**71**	72	**72**	73	cm
28	**28**	28¹/₂	**28¹/₂**	28¹/₂	in

Sleeve length to underarm
Tunic

45	**45**	46	**46**	46	cm
17¹/₂	**17¹/₂**	18	**18**	18	in

Jacket

48	**48**	49	**49**	49	cm
19	**19**	19¹/₂	**19¹/₂**	19¹/₂	in

Jaeger Matchmaker Merino DK
Tunic

12	**12**	13	**13**	14	50 gm

Jacket

14	**15**	15	**16**	17	50 gm

Jaeger Extra Fine Merino DK (941)
Tunic

11	**12**	12	**13**	13	50 gm

Jacket

14	**14**	15	**16**	16	50 gm

Quantities of yarn are approximate as they are based on average requirements. Check actual yarn colour - as printing may not match yarn exactly.

Matchmaker Merino DK versions: Pair each of 3¹/₄ mm (UK 10/USA 3) and 4 mm (UK 8/ USA 6) needles.
Extra Fine Merino DK versions: Pair each of 3 mm (UK 11/USA 2/3) and 3³/₄ mm (UK 9/ USA 5) needles.
Both versions: 5 buttons for Jacket.

Tension
Matchmaker Merino DK versions: 22 sts and 30 rows to 10 cm (stocking st) on 4 mm (USA 6) needles or size needed to achieve stated tension.
Extra Fine Merino DK versions: 22 sts and 32 rows to 10 cm (stocking st) on 3³/₄ mm (USA 5) needles or size needed to achieve stated tension.

For notes and abbreviations, see page 58.

Special note
All decreases (and increases) are worked 4 (and 3) sts in from ends of rows, as follows:
To dec at beg of RS rows: K4, K2tog, K to end.
To dec at ends of RS rows: K to last 6 sts, sL1K, K1, psso, K4.
To inc at beg of RS rows: K3, M1 (**by picking up horizontal loop lying before next st and working into back of it**), K to end.
To inc at ends of RS rows: K to last 3 sts, M1, K3.

TUNIC
BACK

With smaller size needles, cast on 109 [**115**, 121, **127**, 133] sts.
Row 1 - (RS), K1, *P1, K1; rep from * to end. This row forms moss st.
Work in moss st for a further 9 rows, inc 1 st at centre of last row and ending with RS facing for next row (110 [**116**, 122, **128**, 134] sts).
Change to larger size needles and starting

with a K row, work in stocking st until Back meas 45 cm, end with RS facing for next row.
Shape armholes
Cast off 5 sts at beg of next 2 rows (100 [**106**, 112, **118**, 124] sts).**
Dec 1 st (see special note) at each end of next and foll 7 alt rows (84 [**90**, 96, **102**, 108] sts).
Work straight until armhole meas 21 [**21**, 22, **22**, 23] cm, ending with RS facing for next row.
Shape shoulders and back neck
Cast off 9 [**9**, 10, **11**, 12] sts at beg of next 2 rows (66 [**72**, 76, **80**, 84] sts).
Next row - (RS), cast off 9 [**9**, 10, **11**, 12] sts, K until there are 12 [**14**, 15, **15**, 16] sts on right needle, turn and work this side first.
Cast off 4 sts at beg of next row.
Cast off rem 8 [**10**, 11, **11**, 12] sts.
With RS facing, rejoin yarn to rem sts, cast off centre 24 [**26**, 26, **28**, 28] sts, K to end. Work to match first side, reversing shapings.

FRONT
Work as Back to **.
Dec 1 st (see special note) at each end of next and foll 3 alt rows (92 [**98**, 104, **110**, 116] sts).
Work 1 row, ending with RS facing for next row.
Divide for front neck
Next row - (RS), K4, K2tog, K34 [**37**, 40, **43**, 46], sL1K, K1, psso, K4, turn and work this side first (44 [**47**, 50, **53**, 56] sts).
Work 1 row. Dec 1 st (see special note) at each end of next and foll 2 alt rows (38 [**41**, 44, **47**, 50] sts). Work 1 row, thus ending with RS facing for next row.
Dec 1 st (see special note) at neck edge **only** of next and foll 5 [**7**, 5, **7**, 6] alt rows, then every foll 4th row until 26 [**28**, 31, **33**, 36] sts rem.
Work straight until Front matches Back to start of shoulder shaping, ending with RS facing for next row.
Shape shoulder
Cast off 9 [**9**, 10, **11**, 12] sts at beg of next and foll alt row. Work 1 row.
Cast off rem 8 [**10**, 11, **11**, 12] sts.
With RS facing, rejoin yarn to rem sts and proceed thus:
Next row - (RS), K4, K2tog, K34 [**37**, 40, **43**, 46], sL1K, K1, psso, K4 (44 [**47**, 50, **53**, 56] sts). Work to match first side, reversing shapings, working an extra row before start of shoulder shaping.

SLEEVES
With smaller size needles, cast on 55 [**55**, 57, **59**, 59] sts.
Work in moss st as on Back for 10 rows, inc 1 st at centre of last row and thus ending with RS facing for next row (56 [**56**, 58, **60**, 60] sts).
Change to larger size needles and starting with a K row, work in stocking st, shaping sides by inc 1 st at each end of next and every foll 6th row to 80 [**80**, 86, **80**, 96] sts, then on every foll 8th row until there are 92 [**92**, 96, **96**, 100] sts.

Work straight until Sleeve meas 45 [**45**, 46, **46**, 46] cm, ending with RS facing for next row.
Shape top
Cast off 5 sts at beg of next 2 rows (82 [**82**, 86, **86**, 90] sts). Dec 1 st (see special note) at each end of next and foll 6 alt rows, thus ending with **WS** facing for next row (68 [**68**, 72, **72**, 76] sts).
Next row - (**WS**), P2tog, P to last 2 sts, P2tog. Cast off rem 66 [**66**, 70, **70**, 74] sts loosely.

MAKE UP
Press carefully following instructions on ball band.
Join right shoulder seam.
Neck Border
With RS facing and smaller needles, **knit up** 44 [**44**, 46, **46**, 48] sts down left side of front neck, **make one** stitch at centre front by picking up horizontal loop lying before next stitch and working into back of it, mark this stitch, **knit up**, 44 [**44**, 46, **46**, 48] sts up right side of front neck, 4 sts down right side of back neck, 24 [**26**, 26, **28**, 28] sts from centre back, then 4 sts up left side of back neck (121 [**123**, 127, **129**, 133] sts).
Next row - (**WS**), (K1, P1) 37 [**38**, 39, **40**, 41] times, K1, P3tog, (K1,P1) to last st, K1.
Next row - (K1,P1) 21[**21**, 22, **22**, 23] times, sl1, K2 tog, psso, (P1, K1) to end.
Cast off in patt, decreasing 2 sts at centre front as before.
Join left shoulder seam and Neck Border.
Place centre of cast-off edge of Sleeves to shoulder seams, then sew Sleeves into armholes, matching shaped edges.
Join side and sleeve seams.

JACKET
BACK
With smaller size needles, cast on 119 [**125**, 131, **137**, 143] sts.
Row 1 - (RS), K1, *P1, K1; rep from * to end. This row forms moss st.
Work in moss st for a further 13 rows, inc 1 st at centre of last row and ending with RS facing for next row (120 [**126**, 132, **138**, 144] sts).
Change to larger size needles and starting with a K row, work in stocking st until Back meas 48 cm, end with RS facing for next row.
Shape armholes
Cast off 5 sts at beg of next 2 rows (110 [**116**, 122, **128**, 134] sts). Dec 1 st (see special note) at each end of next and foll 7 alt rows (94 [**100**, 106, **112**, 118] sts).
Work straight until armhole meas 23 [**23**, 24, **24**, 25] cm, ending with RS facing for next row.
Shape shoulders and back neck
Cast off 10 [**11**, 12, **12**, 13] sts at beg of next 2 rows (74 [**78**, 82, **88**, 92] sts).
Next row - (RS), cast off 10 [**11**, 12, **12**, 13] sts, K until there are 14 [**14**, 15, **17**, 18] sts on right needle, turn and work this side first.
Cast off 4 sts at beg of next row.
Cast off rem 10 [**10**, 11, **13**, 14] sts.

With RS facing, rejoin yarn to rem sts, cast off centre 26 [**28**, 28, **30**, 30] sts, K to end. Work to match first side, reversing shapings.

POCKET LININGS (Make 2)
With larger size needles, cast on 30 sts.
Starting with a K row, work in stocking st for 40 rows, ending with RS facing for next row. Break yarn and leave sts on a spare needle.

LEFT FRONT
With smaller size needles, cast on 67 [**69**, 73, **75**, 79] sts.
Work in moss st as on Back for 13 rows, thus ending with **WS** facing for next row.
81, 91 and 102 cm sizes:
Next row - (**WS**), patt 8 sts and slip these 8 sts onto a safety pin for Button Border, M1, patt to end (60 [66, 72] sts).
86 and 97 cm sizes:
Next row - (**WS**), patt 8 sts and slip these 8 sts onto a safety pin for Button Border, M1, patt to last st, inc in last st ([**63**, **69**] sts).
All sizes: Change to larger size needles and starting with a K row, work in stocking st until Left Front meas 20 cm, ending with RS facing for next row.
Place pocket
Next row - (RS), K18 [**20**, 22, **24**, 26], slip next 30 sts onto a spare needle and, in their place, K across 30 sts of first Pocket Lining, K12 [**13**, 14, **15**, 16].
Cont straight until 8 rows less have been worked than on Back to start of armhole shaping, ending with RS facing for next row.
Shape front slope
Dec 1 st (see special note) at end of next and foll 4th row (58 [**61**, 64, **67**, 70] sts).
Work 3 rows, end with RS facing for next row.
Shape armhole
Cast off 5 sts at beg and dec 1 st (see special note) at end of next row (52 [**55**, 58, **61**, 64] sts). Work 1 row, thus ending with RS facing for next row.
Working all decreases as set, dec 1 st at armhole edge of next and foll 7 alt rows **and at same time** dec 1 st at front slope edge on every foll 4th row from previous dec (40 [**43**, 46, **49**, 52] sts).
Dec 1 st at front slope edge **only** on every foll 4th row from previous dec until 30 [**32**, 35, **37**, 40] sts rem.
Work straight until Left Front matches Back to start of shoulder shaping, ending with RS facing for next row.
Shape shoulder
Cast off 10 [**11**, 12, **12**, 13] sts at beg of next and foll alt row.
Work 1 row.
Cast off rem 10 [**10**, 11, **13**, 14] sts.

RIGHT FRONT
With smaller size needles, cast on 67 [**69**, 73, **75**, 79] sts.

Work in moss st as on Back for 13 rows, thus ending with **WS** facing for next row.
81, 91 and 102 cm sizes:
Next row - (WS), patt to last 8 sts, M1, turn and slip last 8 sts onto a safety pin for Buttonhole Border (60 [66, 72] sts).
86 and 97 cm sizes:
Next row - (**WS**), inc in first st, patt to last 8 sts, M1, turn and slip last 8 sts onto a safety pin for Buttonhole Border ([**63**, **69**] sts).
All sizes: Change to larger size needles and starting with a K row, work in stocking st until Right Front meas 20 cm, ending with RS facing for next row.
Place pocket
Next row - (RS), K12 [**13**, 14, **15**, 16], slip next 30 sts onto a spare needle and, in their place, K across 30 sts of second Pocket Lining, K18 [**20**, 22, **24**, 26].
Complete to match Left Front, reversing shapings, working an extra row before start of armhole and shoulder shaping.

SLEEVES
With smaller size needles, cast on 61 [**61**, 63, **65**, 65] sts.
Work in moss st as on Back for 14 rows, inc 1 st at centre of last row and thus ending with RS facing for next row (62 [**62**, 64, **66**, 66] sts).
Change to larger size needles, starting with a K row, work in stocking st, shaping sides by inc 1 st at each end of next and every foll 6th [**6th**, 6th, **6th**, 4th] row to 96 [**96**, 104, **98**, 72] sts, then on every foll 8th [**8th**, 8th, **8th**, 6th] row until there are 102 [**102**, 106, **106**, 110] sts.
Work straight until Sleeve meas 48 [**48**, 49, **49**, 49] cm, ending with RS facing for next row.
Shape top
Cast off 5 sts at beg of next 2 rows (92 [**92**, 96, **96**, 100] sts). Dec 1 st (see special note) at each end of next and foll 6 alt rows, end with **WS** facing for next row (78 [**78**, 82, **82**, 86] sts).
Next row - (**WS**), P2tog tbl, P to last 2 sts, P2tog.
Cast off rem 76 [**76**, 80, **80**, 84] sts loosely.

MAKE UP
Press carefully following instructions on ball band. Join both shoulder seams.
Button Border
Slip 8 sts left on Left Front safety pin onto smaller size needles and rejoin yarn with RS facing.
Cont in moss st as set until Border, when slightly stretched, fits up left front opening edge to start of front slope shaping, up front slope and across to centre back neck, sewing in place as you go along and ending with RS facing for next row. Cast off in patt.
Mark positions for 5 buttons on this Border with pins to ensure even spacing - lowest button to be 15 cm above cast-on edge, top button 1.5 cm below start of front slope shaping and rem 3 buttons evenly spaced between.

Buttonhole Border

Slip 8 sts left on Right Front safety pin onto smaller size needles and rejoin yarn with **WS** facing.

Cont in moss st as set until Border, when slightly stretched, fits up right front opening edge to start of front slope shaping, up front slope and across to centre back neck, with the addition of 5 buttonholes to correspond with positions marked for buttons, sewing in place as you go along and ending with RS facing for next row. Cast off in patt.

To make a buttonhole: (RS), patt 2 sts, work 2 tog, (yrn) twice (to make a buttonhole - drop extra loop on next row), patt 4 sts.

Join ends of borders at centre back neck.

Pocket Tops

Slip 30 sts left on spare needle onto smaller size needles and rejoin yarn with RS facing. Work in moss st as on Back for 6 rows, inc 1 st at centre of first row (31 sts). Cast off in patt. Sew Pocket Linings in place on inside and sew down ends of Pocket Tops.

Place centre of cast-off edge of Sleeves to shoulder seams, then sew Sleeves into armholes, matching shaped edges. Join side and sleeve seams. Sew on buttons.

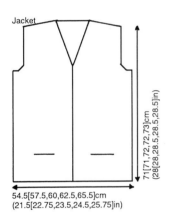

Jacket

54.5[57.5,60,62.5,65.5]cm
(21.5[22.75,23.5,24.5,25.75]in)

71[71,72,72,73]cm
(28[28,28.5,28.5,28.5]in)

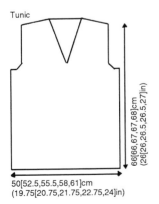

Tunic

50[52.5,55.5,58,61]cm
(19.75[20.75,21.75,22.75,24]in)

66[66,67,67,68]cm
(26[26,26.5,26.5,27]in)

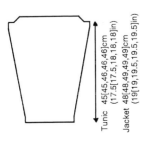

Tunic 45[45,46,46,46]cm
(17.5[17.5,18,18,18]in)

Jacket 48[48,49,49,49]cm
(19[19,19.5,19.5,19.5]in)

Design 7

Cloud

To fit bust					
81	**86**	91	**97**	102	cm
32	**34**	36	**38**	40	in
Actual size					
107	**113**	120	**127**	133	cm
42	**44½**	47	**50**	52½	in
Finished length					
71	**71**	72	**72**	73	cm
28	**28**	28½	**28½**	28½	in
Sleeve length to underarm					
46	**46**	47	**47**	47	cm
18	**18**	18½	**18½**	18½	in
Jaeger Matchmaker Merino DK					
15	**15**	16	**17**	18	50 gm
Jaeger Extra Fine Merino DK (940)					
14	**15**	16	**17**	17	50 gm

Quantities of yarn are approximate as they are based on average requirements.

Check actual yarn colour - as printing may not match yarn exactly.

Matchmaker Merino DK version: Pair each of 3¼ mm (UK 10/USA 3) and 4 mm (UK 8/USA 6) needles.
3¼ mm (UK 10/USA 3) circular needle.
Extra Fine Merino DK version: Pair each of 3 mm (UK 11/USA 2/3) and 3¾ mm (UK 9/USA 5) needles.
3 mm (UK 11/USA 2/3) circular needle.
Both versions: Cable pin.

Tension

Matchmaker Merino DK version: 24 sts and 30 rows to 10 cm (patt when pressed), 22 sts and 30 rows to 10 cm (stocking st) on 4 mm (USA 6) needles or size needed to achieve stated tension.

Extra Fine Merino DK version: 24 sts and 32 rows to 10 cm (patt when pressed), 22 sts and 32 rows to 10 cm (stocking st) on 3¾ mm (USA 5) needles or size needed to achieve stated tension.

For notes and abbreviations, see page 58.

Special note

Cable patt should follow through into rib on Neck Border. Before leaving centre front and back sts on spare needle, make a note of which patt row has just been worked. Depending on which row has just been worked, central 12 sts are decreased down to 10 sts on pick-up row of Neck Border as follows:

After patt rows 10, 12, 14, 16, 18, 20, 22, 24, 26, 28 or 30: P2, (K1 tbl) twice, (P2tog) twice, (K1 tbl) twice, P2.

After patt rows 2 or 8: P1, P2tog, (K1 tbl) twice, P2, (K1 tbl) twice, P2tog, P1.

After patt rows 4 or 6: P1, P2tog, Cr3R, Cr3L, P2tog, P1.

Special abbreviations

C4F=slip next 2 sts on cable pin and leave at front of work, (K1 tbl) twice, then (K1 tbl) twice from cable pin.

Cr3L=slip next 2 sts on cable pin and leave at front of work, P1, then (K1 tbl) twice from cable pin.

Cr3R=slip next st on cable pin and leave at back of work, (K1 tbl) twice, then P1 from cable pin.

BACK

With smaller size needles, cast on 118 [**126**, 134, **142**, 150] sts.

Rib row 1 - (RS), (K1 tbl) twice, *P2, (K1 tbl) twice; rep from * to end.

Rib row 2 - (P1 tbl) twice, *K2, (P1 tbl) twice; rep from * to end.

Rep last 2 rows 3 times more and then row 1 again, thus ending with **WS** facing for next row.

Increase row - (**WS**), rib 18 [**22**, 26, **30**, 34], *M1 (**by picking up horizontal loop lying before next st and working into back of it**), rib 2, M1, rib 18; rep from * 3 times more, M1, rib 2, M1, rib 18 [**22**, 26, **30**, 34] (128 [**136**, 144, **152**, 160] sts).

Change to larger size needles.

Keeping rib correct, **patt** thus:

Row 1 - (RS), rib 16 [**20**, 24, **28**, 32], *Cr3L, P2, Cr3R, rib 14; rep from * 3 times more, Cr3L, P2, Cr3R, rib 16 [**20**, 24, **28**, 32].

Row 2 - Rib 16 [**20**, 24, **28**, 32], *K1, (P1 tbl) twice, K2, (P1 tbl) twice, K1, rib 14; rep from * 3 times more, K1, (P1 tbl) twice, K2, (P1 tbl) twice, K1, rib 16 [**20**, 24, **28**, 32].

Row 3 - Rib 16 [**20**, 24, **28**, 32], *P1, Cr3R, P1, rib 14; rep from * 3 times more, P1, Cr3L, Cr3R, P1, rib 16 [**20**, 24, **28**, 32].

Row 4 - Rib 16 [**20**, 24, **28**, 32], *K2, (P1 tbl) 4 times, K2, rib 14; rep from * 3 times more, K2, (P1 tbl) 4 times, K2, rib 16 [**20**, 24, **28**, 32].

Row 5 - Rib 16 [**20**, 24, **28**, 32], *P2, C4F, P2, rib 14; rep from * 3 times more, P2, C4F, P2, rib 16 [**20**, 24, **28**, 32].

Row 6 - As row 4.

Row 7 - Rib 16 [**20**, 24, **28**, 32], *P1, Cr3R, Cr3L, P1, rib 14; rep from * 3 times more, P1, Cr3R, Cr3L, P1, rib 16 [**20**, 24, **28**, 32].

Row 8 - As row 2.

Row 9 - Rib 16 [**20**, 24, **28**, 32], *Cr3R, P2, Cr3L, rib 14; rep from * 3 times more, Cr3R, P2, Cr3L, rib 16 [**20**, 24, **28**, 32].

Row 10 - Rib 16 [**20**, 24, **28**, 32], *(P1 tbl) twice, K4, (P1 tbl) twice, rib 14; rep from * 3 times more, (P1 tbl) twice, K4, (P1 tbl) twice, rib 16 [**20**, 24, **28**, 32].

Row 11 - Rib 16 [**20**, 24, **28**, 32], *(K1 tbl) twice, P4, (K1 tbl) twice, rib 14; rep from * 3 times more, (K1 tbl) twice, P4, (K1 tbl) twice, rib 16 [**20**, 24, **28**, 32].

Rows 12 to 29 - As rows 10 and 11, 9 times.

Row 30 - As row 10.

These 30 rows form patt.

Cont in patt until Back meas 48 cm, ending with RS facing for next row.

Shape armholes

Keeping patt correct, cast off 6 sts at beg of next 2 rows (116 [**124**, 132, **140**, 148] sts).

Dec 1 st at each end of next and foll 7 alt rows (100 [**108**, 116, **124**, 132] sts).

Work straight until armhole meas 23 [**23**, 24, **24**, 25] cm, ending with RS facing for next row.

Shape shoulders and back neck

Keeping patt correct, cast off 10 [**11**, 13, **14**, 15] sts at beg of next 2 rows (80 [**86**, 90, **96**, 102] sts).

Next row - (RS), cast off 10 [**11**, 13, **14**, 15] sts, patt until there are 14 [**16**, 16, **18**, 20] sts on right needle, turn and work this side first.

Cast off 4 sts at beg of next row.

Cast off rem 10 [**12**, 12, **14**, 16] sts.

With RS facing, slip centre 32 sts onto a spare needle (see special note), rejoin yarn to rem sts, patt to end.

Work to match first side, reversing shapings.

FRONT

Work as Back until 14 rows less have been worked before start of shoulder and back neck shaping, thus ending with RS facing for next row.

Shape front neck

Next row - (RS), patt 38 [**42**, 46, **50**, 54], turn and work this side first.

Keeping patt correct, cast off 4 sts at beg of next row (34 [**38**, 42, **46**, 50] sts). Dec 1 st at neck edge on next 4 rows (30 [**34**, 38, **42**, 46] sts). Work 8 rows, thus ending with RS facing for next row.

Shape shoulder

Cast off 10 [**11**, 13, **14**, 15] sts at beg of next and foll alt row.

Work 1 row.

Cast off rem 10 [**12**, 12, **14**, 16] sts.

With RS facing, slip centre 24 sts onto a spare needle (see special note), rejoin yarn to rem sts, patt to end.

Work to match first side, reversing shapings, working an extra row before start of shoulder shaping.

SLEEVES

With smaller size needles, cast on 58 [**58**, 58, **66**, 66] sts.

Work in rib as on Back for 9 rows, thus ending with **WS** facing for next row

Increase row - (WS), rib 18 [**18**, 18, **22**, 22], M1, rib 2, M1, rib 18, M1, rib 2, M1, rib 18 [**18**, 18, **22**, 22]

(62 [**62**, 62, **70**, 70] sts).

Change to larger size needles.

Keeping rib correct, **patt** thus:

Row 1 - (RS), inc in first st, rib 15 [**15**, 15, **19**, 19], *Cr3L, P2, Cr3R*, rib 14, rep from * to * once more, rib 15 [**15**, 15, **19**, 19], inc in last st (64 [**64**, 64, **72**, 72] sts).

Row 2 - Rib 17 [**17**, 17, **21**, 21], *K1, (P1 tbl) twice, K2, (P1 tbl) twice, K1*, rib 14, rep from * to * once more, rib 17 [**17**, 17, **21**, 21].

Row 3 - Rib 17 [**17**, 17, **21**, 21], *P1, Cr3L, Cr3R, P1*, rib 14, rep from * to * once more, rib 17 [**17**, 17, **21**, 21].

Row 4 - Rib 17 [**17**, 17, **21**, 21], *K2, (P1 tbl) 4 times, K2*, rib 14, rep from * to * once more, rib 17 [**17**, 17, **21**, 21].

Row 5 - Inc in first st, rib 16 [**16**, 16, **20**, 20], *P2, C4F, P2*, rib 14, rep from * to * once more, rib 16 [**16**, 16, **20**, 20], inc in last st (66 [**66**, 66, **74**, 74] sts).

Row 6 - Rib 18 [**18**, 18, **22**, 22], *K2, (P1 tbl) 4 times, K2*, rib 14, rep from * to * once more, rib 18 [**18**, 18, **22**, 22].

These 6 rows set position of patt as on Back and set sleeve seam shaping.

Cont in patt, shaping sides by inc 1 st at each end of every foll 4th row **from previous inc** to 84 [**84**, 94, **78**, 90] sts, then on every foll 6th row until there are 110 [**110**, 114, **114**, 118] sts, taking inc sts into rib.

Work straight until Sleeve meas 46 [**46**, 47, **47**, 47] cm, ending with RS facing for next row.

Shape top

Keeping patt correct, cast off 6 sts at beg of next 2 rows (98 [**98**, 102, **102**, 106] sts).

Dec 1 st at each end of next and foll 6 alt rows, thus ending with **WS** facing for next row (84 [**84**, 88, **88**, 92] sts).

Dec 1 st at each end of next row.

Cast off rem 82 [**82**, 86, **86**, 90] sts in patt.

MAKE UP

Pin out pieces to measurements given and steam press firmly to set rib. Allow to dry naturally before completing make up.

Join both shoulder seams.

Neck Border

With RS facing and circular needle, starting at left shoulder seam, **knit up** 21 sts down left side of front neck, patt 24 sts from front as follows: rib 6, work next 12 sts as detailed in special note, rib 6, **knit up** 21 sts up right side of front neck, 5 sts down right side of back neck, patt 32 sts from back as follows: rib 10, work next 12 sts as detailed in special note, rib 10, then **knit up** 5 sts up left side of back neck (104 sts).

Working in rounds, not rows, proceed thus:

Next round - (RS), *P1, (K1 tbl) twice, P1; rep from * to end.

Rep last round for 8 cm.

Cast off loosely and evenly in rib.

Place centre of cast-off edge of Sleeves to shoulder seams, then sew Sleeves into armholes, matching shaped edges.

Join side and sleeve seams.

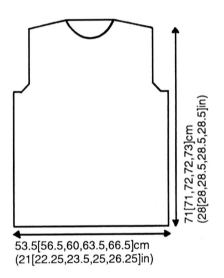

71[71,72,72,73]cm
(28[28,28.5,28.5,28.5]in)

53.5[56.5,60,63.5,66.5]cm
(21[22.25,23.5,25,26.25]in)

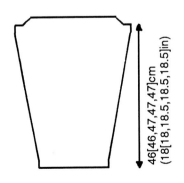

46[46,47,47,47]cm
(18[18,18.5,18.5,18.5]in)

Design 8

Mull

To fit bust

81	**86**	91	**97**	102	cm
32	**34**	36	**38**	40	in

Actual size, at underarm

110	**116**	121	**126**	131	cm
43¹/₂	**45¹/₂**	47¹/₂	**49¹/₂**	51¹/₂	in

Finished length

72	**72**	73	**73**	74	cm
28¹/₂	**28¹/₂**	28¹/₂	**28¹/₂**	29	in

Sleeve length to underarm

44	**44**	44	**44**	44	cm
17¹/₂	**17¹/₂**	17¹/₂	**17¹/₂**	17¹/₂	in

Jaeger Shetland Aran (013)

12	**13**	13	**14**	14	100 gm

Jaeger Matchmaker Merino Aran

24	**25**	26	**27**	28	50 gm

Quantities of yarn are approximate as they are based on average requirements. Check actual yarn colour - as printing may not match yarn exactly.

Pair each of 4 mm (UK 8/USA 6) and 4¹/₂ mm (UK 7/USA 7) needles.
Cable pin.
7 buttons.

Tension
23 sts and 32 rows to 10 cm (patt), 18 sts and 25 rows to 10 cm (stocking st) on 4¹/₂ mm (USA 7) needles or size needed to achieve stated tension.

For notes and abbreviations, see page 58.

Special note
When casting off, dec 2 sts across top of each cable panel. St counts given are prior to these decreases.

Special abbreviations
M1P=make a st by picking up horizontal loop lying before next st and purling into back of it
C8F=slip next 4 sts on cable pin and leave at front of work, K4, then K4 from cable pin.
C8B=slip next 4 sts on cable pin and leave at back of work, K4, then K4 from cable pin.

BACK
With 4 mm (USA 6) needles, cast on 95 [**101**, 107, **113**, 119] sts.
Row 1 - (RS), P1 [**0**, 1, **0**, 1], (K1, P1) 3 [**5**, 6, **8**, 9] times, *K4, (P1, K1) 3 times, P1; rep from * to last 0 [**3**, 6, **9**, 12] sts, (K1, P1) 0 [**1**, 3, **4**, 6] times, K0 [**1**, 0, **1**, 0].
Row 2 - P1 [**0**, 1, **0**, 1], (K1, P1) 3 [**5**, 6, **8**, 9] times, *P4, (P1, K1) 3 times, P1; rep from * to last 0 [**3**, 6, **9**, 12] sts, (K1, P1) 0 [**1**, 3, **4**, 6] times, K0 [**1**, 0, **1**, 0].
Row 3 - As row 1.
Row 4 - P1 [**0**, 1, **0**, 1], (K1, P1) 3 [**5**, 6, **8**, 9] times, *(P1, M1P **by picking up horizontal loop lying before next st and purling into back of it**) 4 times, (P1, K1) 3 times, P1; rep from * to last 0 [**3**, 6, **9**, 12] sts, (K1, P1) 0 [**1**, 3, **4**, 6] times, K0 [**1**, 0, **1**, 0]
(127 [**133**, 139, **145**, 151] sts).
Patt thus:
Row 1 - (RS), P1 [**0**, 1, **0**, 1], (K1, P1) 3 [**5**, 6, **8**, 9] times, *C8F, (P1, K1) 3 times, P1, C8B, (P1, K1) 3 times, P1; rep from * to last 0 [**3**, 6, **9**, 12] sts, (K1, P1) 0 [**1**, 3, **4**, 6] times, K0 [**1**, 0, **1**, 0].
Row 2 and every foll alt row - P1 [**0**, 1, **0**, 1], (K1, P1) 3 [**5**, 6, **8**, 9] times, *P8, (P1, K1) 3 times, P1; rep from * to last 0 [**3**, 6, **9**, 12] sts, (K1, P1) 0 [**1**, 3, **4**, 6] times, K0 [**1**, 0, **1**, 0].
Rows 3, 5, 7 and 9 - P1 [**0**, 1, **0**, 1], (K1, P1) 3 [**5**, 6, **8**, 9] times, *K8, (P1, K1) 3 times, P1; rep from * to last 0 [**3**, 6, **9**, 12] sts, (K1, P1) 0 [**1**, 3, **4**, 6] times, K0 [**1**, 0, **1**, 0].
Row 10 - As row 2.
These 10 rows form patt.
Work in patt for a further 6 rows, thus ending with RS facing for next row.
Change to 4¹/₂ mm (USA 7) needles and cont in patt until Back meas approx 47 cm, ending after patt row 8 and with RS facing for next row.
Shape raglans
Keeping patt correct, cast off 6 [**9**, 9, **9**, 9] sts at beg of next 2 rows
(115 [**115**, 121, **127**, 133] sts).
91, 97 and 102 cm sizes: Dec 1 st at each end of next [**3**, **6**, 9] rows
(115 sts).
97 cm size:
Next row - (RS), patt 9, P2tog, patt to last 11 sts, P2tog, patt 9
(113 sts).
91, 97 and 102 cm sizes:
Next row - (WS), P9, K2tog, patt to last 11 sts, K2tog, P9.
Next row - Patt 9, P2tog, patt to last 11 sts, P2tog, patt 9.

Rep last 2 rows [0, **0**, 1] times more
([111, **109**, 107] sts).
Next row - P9, patt to last 9 sts, P9.
All sizes
Next row - (RS), patt 9, P2tog, patt to last 11 sts, P2tog, patt 9.
Next row - P9, patt to last 9 sts, P9.
Rep last 2 rows 38 [**38**, 36, **35**, 34] times more.
Decreasing sts as required (see special note), cast off rem 37 sts.

POCKET LININGS (Make 2)
With 4¹/₂ mm (USA 7) needles cast on 33 sts.
Row 1 - (RS), (P1, K1) twice, P1, K8, (P1, K1) 3 times, P1, K8, (P1, K1) twice, P1.
Row 2 - (P1, K1) twice, P9, (P1, K1) 3 times, P9, (P1, K1) twice, P1.
Rep last 2 rows 19 times more, thus ending with RS facing for next row.
Break yarn and leave sts on a spare needle.

LEFT FRONT
With 4 mm (USA 6) needles, cast on 51 [**54**, 57, **60**, 63] sts.
Row 1 - (RS), P1 [**0**, 1, **0**, 1], (K1, P1) 3 [**5**, 6, **8**, 9] times, *K4, (P1, K1) 3 times, P1; rep from * to end.
Row 2 - *P1, (K1, P1) 3 times, P4; rep from * to last 7 [**10**, 13, **16**, 19] sts, (P1, K1) 3 [**5**, 6, **8**, 9] times, P1 [**0**, 1, **0**, 1].
Row 3 - As row 1.
Row 4 - *P1, (K1, P1) 3 times, (P1, M1P) 4 times; rep from * to last 7 [**10**, 13, **16**, 19] sts, (P1, K1) 3 [**5**, 6, **8**, 9] times, P1 [**0**, 1, **0**, 1]
(67 [**70**, 73, **76**, 79] sts).
Patt thus:
Row 1 - (RS), P1 [**0**, 1, **0**, 1], (K1, P1) 3 [**5**, 6, **8**, 9] times, *C8F, (P1, K1) 3 times, P1, C8B, (P1, K1) 3 times, P1; rep from * once more.
Row 2 and every foll alt row - *(P1, K1) 3 times, P9; rep from * to last 7 [**10**, 13, **16**, 19] sts, (P1, K1) 3 [**5**, 6, **8**, 9] times, P1 [**0**, 1, **0**, 1].
Rows 3, 5, 7 and 9 - P1 [**0**, 1, **0**, 1], (K1, P1) 3 [**5**, 6, **8**, 9] times, *K8, (P1, K1) 3 times, P1; rep from * to end.
Row 10 - As row 2.
These 10 rows form patt.
Work in patt for a further 5 rows, thus ending with **WS** facing for next row.
Next row - (WS), patt 7 and slip these 7 sts onto a safety pin, M1 (**by picking up horizontal loop lying before next st and working into back of it**), patt to end (61 [**64**, 67, **70**, 73] sts).
Change to 4¹/₂ mm (USA 7) needles and cont in patt for a further 40 rows, thus ending after patt row 6 and with RS facing for next row.
Place pocket
Next row - (RS), patt 17 [**20**, 23, **26**, 29], slip next 33 sts onto a spare needle and, in their place, patt across 33 sts of first Pocket Lining, patt 11.
Work straight until Left Front matches Back to start of raglan shaping, ending after patt row 8 and with RS facing for next row.

81 and 86 cm sizes
Shape raglan and front slope
Keeping patt correct, cast off 6 [**9**] sts at beg and dec 1 st at end of next row (54 sts). Work 1 row, thus ending with RS facing for next row. Working raglan decreases 9 sts in from raglan edge as set by Back, dec 1 st at raglan edge on next and every foll alt row **and at same time** dec 1 st at front slope edge on every foll 4th row from previous dec until 9 sts rem.

91, 97 and 102 cm sizes
Shape raglan
Keeping patt correct, cast off 9 sts at beg of next row ([**58**, **61**, 64] sts). Work 1 row, thus ending with RS facing for next row.
Dec 1 st at raglan edge of next [0, **2**, 4] rows ([**58**, **59**, 60] sts).
Shape front slope
Dec 1 st at each end of next row ([**56**, **57**, 58] sts).
Working raglan decreases as set by Back, dec 1 st at raglan edge on next [4, **6**, 8] rows, then on every foll alt row **and at same time** dec 1 st at front slope edge on every foll 4th row from previous dec until 9 sts rem.
All sizes: Work 1 row, thus ending with RS facing for next row.
Next row - (RS), P1, K6, K2tog (8 sts).
Next row - P8.
Next row - P1, K4, K3tog (6 sts).
Next row - P6.
Next row - P1, K3, K2tog (5 sts).
Next row - P5.
Next row - P1, K1, K3tog (3 sts).
Next row - P3.
Next row - P1, K2tog (2sts).
Next row - P2.
Next row - K2tog and fasten off.

RIGHT FRONT
With 4 mm (USA 6) needles, cast on 51 [**54**, 57, **60**, 63] sts.
Row 1 - (RS), *P1, (K1, P1) 3 times, K4; rep from * to last 7 [**10**, 13, **16**, 19] sts, (P1, K1) 3 [**5**, 6, **8**, 9] times, P1 [**0**, 1, **0**, 1].
Row 2 - P1 [**0**, 1, **0**, 1], (K1, P1) 3 [**5**, 6, **8**, 9] times, *P4, (P1, K1) 3 times, P1; rep from * to end.
Row 3 - As row 1.
Row 4 - P1 [**0**, 1, **0**, 1], (K1, P1) 3 [**5**, 6, **8**, 9] times, *(P1, M1P) 4 times, (P1, K1) 3 times, P1; rep from * to end (67 [**70**, 73, **76**, 79] sts).
Patt thus:
Row 1 - (RS), *P1, (K1, P1) 3 times, C8F, P1, (K1, P1) 3 times, C8B; rep from * once more, (P1, K1) 3 [**5**, 6, **8**, 9] times, P1 [**0**, 1, **0**, 1].
Row 2 and every foll alt row - P1 [**0**, 1, **0**, 1], (K1, P1) 3 [**5**, 6, **8**, 9] times, *P9, (K1, P1) 3 times; rep from * to end.
Rows 3, 5, 7 and 9 - *P1, (K1, P1) 3 times, K8; rep from * 3 times more, (P1, K1) 3 [**5**, 6, **8**, 9] times, P1 [**0**, 1, **0**, 1].
Row 10 - As row 2.
These 10 rows form patt.

Next row - (RS), P1, K1, P1, (yrn) twice (to make a buttonhole - drop extra loop on next row), P2tog, patt to end.
Work in patt for a further 4 rows, thus ending with **WS** facing for next row.
Next row - (**WS**), patt to last 7 sts, M1 and turn, leaving last 7 sts on a safety pin (61 [**64**, 67, **70**, 73] sts).
Change to 4¹/₂ mm (USA 7) needles and cont in patt for a further 40 rows, thus ending after patt row 6 and with RS facing for next row.
Place pocket
Next row - (RS), patt 11, slip next 33 sts onto a spare needle and, in their place, patt across 33 sts of second Pocket Lining, patt 17 [**20**, 23, **26**, 29].
Complete to match Left Front, reversing shapings, working an extra row before start of raglan shaping.

LEFT SLEEVE
With 4 mm (USA 6) needles, cast on 49 [**49**, 51, **51**, 53] sts.
Row 1 - (RS), P0 [**0**, 1, **1**, 0], (K1, P1) 3 [**3**, 3, **3**, 4] times, *K4, (P1, K1) 3 times, P1; rep from * to last 10 [**10**, 11, **11**, 12] sts, K4, (P1, K1) 3 [**3**, 3, **3**, 4] times, P0 [**0**, 1, **1**, 0].
Row 2 - P0 [**0**, 1, **1**, 0], (K1, P1) 3 [**3**, 3, **3**, 4] times, *P4, (P1, K1) 3 times, P1; rep from * to last 10 [**10**, 11, **11**, 12] sts, P4, (P1, K1) 3 [**3**, 3, **3**, 4] times, P0 [**0**, 1, **1**, 0].
Row 3 - As row 1.
Row 4 - P0 [**0**, 1, **1**, 0], (K1, P1) 3 [**3**, 3, **3**, 4] times, *(P1, M1P) 4 times, (P1, K1) 3 times, P1; rep from * to last 10 [**10**, 11, **11**, 12] sts, (P1, M1P) 4 times, (P1, K1) 3 [**3**, 3, **3**, 4] times, P0 [**0**, 1, **1**, 0] (65 [**65**, 67, **67**, 69] sts).
Patt thus:
Row 1 - (RS), P0 [**0**, 1, **1**, 0], (K1, P1) 3 [**3**, 3, **3**, 4] times, C8B, (P1, K1) 3 times, P1, C8F, (P1, K1) 3 times, P1, C8B, (P1, K1) 3 times, P1, C8F, (P1, K1) 3 [**3**, 3, **3**, 4] times, P0 [**0**, 1, **1**, 0].
Row 2 and every foll alt row - P0 [**0**, 1, **1**, 0], (K1, P1) 3 [**3**, 3, **3**, 4] times, *P8, (P1, K1) 3 times, P1; rep from * to last 14 [**14**, 15, **15**, 16] sts, P8, (P1, K1) 3 [**3**, 3, **3**, 4] times, P0 [**0**, 1, **1**, 0].
Rows 3, 5, 7 and 9 - P0 [**0**, 1, **1**, 0], (K1, P1) 3 [**3**, 3, **3**, 4] times, *K8, (P1, K1) 3 times, P1; rep from * to last 14 [**14**, 15, **15**, 16] sts, K8, (P1, K1) 3 [**3**, 3, **3**, 4] times, P0 [**0**, 1, **1**, 0].
Row 10 - As row 2.
These 10 rows form patt.
Work a further 6 rows in patt, thus ending with RS facing for next row.
Change to 4¹/₂ mm (USA 7) needles and cont in patt, shaping sides by inc 1 st at each end of 5th [**3rd**, 3rd, **3rd**, 3rd] and every foll 6th [**6th**, 4th, **4th**, 4th] row until there are 81 [**103**, 81, **99**, 113] sts, taking inc sts into patt.
81, 91, 97 and 102 cm sizes: Inc 1 st at each end of every foll 8th [**6th**, **6th**, 6th] row from previous inc until there are 97 [109, **115**, 121] sts.

All sizes: Work straight until Sleeve meas approx 44 cm, ending after patt row 8 and with RS facing for next row.
Shape raglan
Keeping patt correct, cast off 6 [**9**, 9, **9**, 9] sts at beg of next 2 rows (85 [**85**, 91, **97**, 103] sts).
81, 86, 91 and 97 sizes: Working raglan decreases as set by Back, dec 1 st at each end of next and every foll 4th row until 71 [**71**, 81, **91**] sts rem. Work 1 row, thus ending with RS facing for next row.
All sizes: Working raglan decreases as set by Back, dec 1 st at each end of next and every foll alt row until 27 sts rem, thus ending with **WS** facing for next row.**
Shape neck
Keeping patt correct and decreasing sts as required (see special note), proceed thus:
Cast off 4 sts at beg of next row.
Next row - (RS), patt 9, P2tog, patt to end.
Rep last 2 rows once more (17 sts).
Cast off 5 sts at beg of next row (12 sts).
Next row - Patt 9, P2tog, patt 1 (11 sts).
Cast off 5 sts at beg of next row (6 sts).
Next row - Patt 4, K2tog (5 sts).
Cast off rem 5 sts.

RIGHT SLEEVE
Work as for Left Sleeve to **.
Shape neck
Keeping patt correct and decreasing sts as required (see special note), proceed thus:
Patt 1 row, ending with RS facing for next row.
Next row - (RS), cast off 4 sts, patt to last 11 sts, P2tog, patt 9.
Rep last 2 rows once more (17 sts).
Patt 1 row.
Next row - Cast off 5 sts (one st on right needle after cast-off), P2tog, patt 9 (11 sts).
Patt 1 row. Cast off 6 sts at beg of next row (5 sts). Patt 1 row. Cast off rem 5 sts.

MAKE UP
Press carefully following instructions on ball band.
Join raglan seams.
Button Border and Left Collar
Slip 7 sts left on Left Front safety pin onto 4 mm (USA 6) needles and rejoin yarn with RS facing.
Cont in moss st as set until Border, when slightly stretched, fits up Left Front to start of front slope shaping, sewing in place as you go along and ending with RS facing for next row.
Shape collar
Inc 1 st at beg (attached inner edge) of next and foll 11 alt rows, then on every foll 4th row until there are 29 sts, taking inc sts into patt.
Cont in moss st as set until Collar fits up left front slope, across top of Left Sleeve and across to centre back neck, sewing in place as you go along and ending at outer (unattached) edge of Collar.
Next row - Patt to last 2 sts, wrap next st (by

slipping next st onto right needle, taking yarn to opposite side of work between needles and then slipping same st back onto left needle), turn and patt to end.

Next row - Patt to last 4 sts, wrap next st, turn and patt to end.

Next row - Patt to last 6 sts, wrap next st, turn and patt to end.

Cont in this way, working 2 less sts on each row, until the foll row has been worked:

Next row - Patt to last 16 sts, wrap next st, turn and patt to end.

Cast off in patt across all sts.

Mark positions for 7 buttons on Button Border section with pins to ensure even spacing - lowest button to be level with buttonhole in Right Front, top button 1 cm below start of front slope shaping and rem 5 buttons evenly spaced between.

Buttonhole Border and Right Collar

Slip 7 sts left on Right Front safety pin onto 4 mm (USA 6) needles and rejoin yarn with **WS** facing.

Cont in moss st as set until Border, when slightly stretched, fits up Right Front to start of front slope shaping, sewing in place as you go along, with the addition of a further 6 buttonholes to correspond with positions marked for buttons and ending with RS facing for next row.

To make a buttonhole (RS): P1, K1, P1, (yrn) twice (to make a buttonhole - drop extra loop on next row), P2tog, K1, P1.

Complete to match Button Border and Left Collar, reversing shaping.

Join ends of Collar sections at centre back neck.

Pocket Tops

Slip 33 sts left on spare needle onto 4 mm (USA 6) needles and rejoin yarn with RS facing.

Work 6 rows in patt as set.

Decreasing sts as required (see special note), cast off in patt.

Sew Pocket Linings in place on inside and sew down ends of Pocket Tops.

Join side and sleeve seams. Sew on buttons.

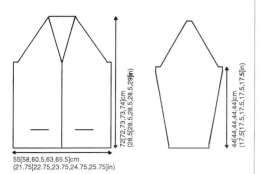

55[58,60.5,63,65.5]cm
(21.75[22.75,23.75,24.75,25.75]in)

72[72,73,73,74]cm
(28.5[28.5,28.5,28.5,29]in)

44[44,44,44,44]cm
(17.5[17.5,17.5,17.5,17.5]in)

Design 9

Allure

To fit bust

81	**86**	91	**97**	102	cm
32	**34**	36	**38**	40	in

Actual size, at underarm

102	**107**	111	**116**	120	cm
40	**42**	43½	**45½**	47	in

Finished length

58	**58**	59	**60**	60	cm
23	**23**	23	**23½**	23½	in

Sleeve length to underarm

46	**46**	47	**47**	47	cm
18	**18**	18½	**18½**	18½	in

Jaeger Matchmaker Merino Aran (761)

12	**13**	13	**14**	15	50 gm

Jaeger Shetland Aran

6	**7**	7	**7**	7	100 gm

Quantities of yarn are approximate as they are based on average requirements.

Check actual yarn colour - as printing may not match yarn exactly.

Pair each of 4 mm (UK 8/USA 6) and 4½ mm (UK 7/USA 7) needles.
8 buttons.

Tension

18 sts and 25 rows to 10 cm (stocking st) on 4½ mm (USA 7) needles or size needed to achieve stated tension.

For notes and abbreviations, see page 58.

Special note

All increases and decreases (**except at sleeve top**) are worked 3 sts in from ends of rows.

To dec at beg of RS rows: K3, K2tog, patt to end.

To dec at ends of RS rows: patt to last 5 sts, K2tog tbl, K3.

To dec at beg of WS rows: P3, P2tog, patt to end.

To dec at ends of WS rows: patt to last 5 sts, P2tog tbl, P3.

To inc at beg of RS rows: K3, M1 (**by picking up horizontal loop lying before next st and working into back of it**), patt to end.

To inc at end of RS rows: patt to last 3 sts, M1, K3.

BACK

With 4 mm (USA 6) needles, cast on 92 [**96**, 100, **104**, 108] sts.

Rib row 1 - (RS), K1, P2 [**0**, 2, **0**, 2], *(K1 tbl) twice, P2; rep from * to last 1 [**3**, 1, **3**, 1] sts, (K1 tbl) 0 [**2**, 0, **2**, 0] times, K1.

Rib row 2 - K3 [**1**, 3, **1**, 3], *(P1 tbl) twice, K2; rep from * to last 1 [**3**, 1, **3**, 1] sts, (P1 tbl) 0 [**2**, 0, **2**, 0] times, K1.

These 2 rows form rib.

Work in rib for a further 22 rows, thus ending with RS facing for next row.

Change to 4½ mm (USA 7) needles and starting with a K row, work in stocking st, shaping side seams (see special note) by dec 1 st at each end of next and every foll 6th row until 82 [**86**, 90, **94**, 98] sts rem.

Work 13 rows, thus ending with RS facing for next row.

Inc 1 st (see special note) at each end of next and every foll 6th row until there are 92 [**96**, 100, **104**, 108] sts.

Work straight until Back meas 38 cm, ending with RS facing for next row.

Shape armholes

Cast off 5 [**6**, 6, **7**, 7] sts at beg of next 2 rows, then 3 [**3**, 4, **4**, 5] sts at beg of foll 2 rows (76 [**78**, 80, **82**, 84] sts).

Dec 1 st at each end of next 3 rows, then on foll 2 alt rows (66 [**68**, 70, **72**, 74] sts).

Work 3 rows, thus ending with RS facing for next row.

Dec 1 st at each end of next and foll 4th row (62 [**64**, 66, **68**, 70] sts).

Work straight until armhole meas 20 [**20**, 21, **22**, 22] cm, ending with RS facing for next row.

Shape shoulders and back neck

Cast off 6 [**7**, 7, **7**, 7] sts at beg of next 2 rows (50 [**50**, 52, **54**, 56] sts).

Next row - (RS), cast off 6 [**7**, 7, **7**, 7] sts, K until there are 11 [**10**, 11, **11**, 12] sts on right needle, turn and work this side first.

Cast off 4 sts at beg of next row.

Cast off rem 7 [**6**, 7, **7**, 8] sts.

With RS facing, rejoin yarn to rem sts, cast off centre 16 [**16**, 16, **18**, 18] sts, K to end. Work to match first side, reversing shapings.

LEFT FRONT

With 4 mm (USA 6) needles, cast on 54 [**56**, 58, **60**, 62] sts.

Rib row 1 - (RS), K1, P2 [**0**, 2, **0**, 2], *(K1 tbl) twice, P2; rep from * to last 3 sts, (K1 tbl) twice, K1.

Rib row 2 - K1, *(P1 tbl) twice, K2; rep from * to last 1 [**3**, 1, **3**, 1] sts, (P1 tbl) 0 [**2**, 0, **2**, 0] times, K1.

These 2 rows form rib.

Work in rib for a further 21 rows, thus ending with **WS** facing for next row.

Row 24 - (WS), patt 8 and slip these 8 sts onto a safety pin for Button Border, patt to end (46 [**48**, 50, **52**, 54] sts).

Change to 4½ mm (USA 7) needles and starting with a K row, work in stocking st, shaping side seam by dec 1 st at beg of next and every foll 6th row until 41 [**43**, 45, **47**, 49] sts rem.

Work 13 rows, thus ending with RS facing for next row.

Inc 1 st at beg of next and every foll 6th row until there are 46 [**48**, 50, **52**, 54] sts.

Work straight until Left Front matches Back to start of armhole shaping, ending with RS facing for next row.

Shape armhole and front slope

Cast off 5 [**6**, 6, **7**, 7] sts at beg and dec 1 st at end of next row (40 [**41**, 43, **44**, 46] sts).

Work 1 row.

Cast off 3 [**3**, 4, **4**, 5] sts at beg of next row (37 [**38**, 39, **40**, 41] sts).

Work 1 row, thus ending with RS facing for next row.

Dec 1 st at armhole edge of next 3 rows, then on foll 2 alt rows **and at same time** dec 1 st at front slope edge on every foll 4th row from previous dec (30 [**31**, 32, **33**, 34] sts).

Work 3 rows, dec 1 st at front slope edge **only** on 4th row from previous dec and thus ending with RS facing for next row (29 [**30**, 31, **32**, 33] sts).

Dec 1 st at armhole edge of next and foll 4th row **and at same time** dec 1 st at front slope edge on 4th row from previous dec (26 [**27**, 28, **29**, 30] sts).

Dec 1 st at front slope edge only on every foll 4th row from previous dec until 19 [**20**, 21, **21**, 22] sts rem.

Work straight until Left Front matches Back to start of shoulder shaping, ending with RS facing for next row.

Shape shoulder

Cast off 6 [**7**, 7, **7**, 7] sts at beg of next and foll alt row. Work 1 row.

Cast off rem 7 [**6**, 7, **7**, 8] sts.

RIGHT FRONT

With 4 mm (USA 6) needles, cast on 54 [**56**, 58, **60**, 62] sts.

Rib row 1 - (RS), K1, *(K1 tbl) twice, P2; rep from * to last 1 [**3**, 1, **3**, 1] sts, (K1 tbl) 0 [**2**, 0, **2**, 0] times, K1.

Rib row 2 - K3 [**1**, 3, **1**, 3], *(P1 tbl) twice, K2; rep from * to last 3 sts, (P1 tbl) twice, K1.

These 2 rows form rib.

Work in rib for a further 2 rows, thus ending with RS facing for next row.

Buttonhole row - (RS), K1, (K1 tbl) twice, P2tog, (yrn) twice (to make a buttonhole - drop extra loop on next row), rib to end.

Rib 7 rows, then rep the **buttonhole row** once more.

Rep last 8 rows once more.

Rib a further 2 rows, thus ending with **WS** facing for next row.

Row 24 - (WS), patt to last 8 sts and turn, leaving last 8 sts on a safety pin for Buttonhole Border (46 [**48**, 50, **52**, 54] sts).

Change to 4½ mm (USA 7) needles and complete to match Left Front, reversing shapings, working an extra row before start of armhole and shoulder shapings.

SLEEVES

With 4 mm (USA 6) needles, cast on 40 [**44**, 44, **48**, 48] sts.

Work in rib as for 81 cm size of Back for 24 rows, thus ending with RS facing for next row.

Change to 4½ mm (USA 7) needles and starting with a K row, work in stocking st, shaping sides by inc 1 st at each end of next and every foll 8th row until there are 62 [**56**, 64, **58**, 68] sts.

86, 91, 97 and 102 cm sizes: Inc 1 st at each end of every foll 10th row from previous inc until there are [**64**, 66, **68**, 70] sts.

All sizes: Work straight until Sleeve meas 46 [**46**, 47, **47**, 47] cm, ending with RS facing for next row.

Shape top

Cast off 4 [**5**, 5, **6**, 6] sts at beg of next 2 rows (54 [**54**, 56, **56**, 58] sts). Dec 1 st at each end of next 3 rows, then on every foll alt row until 44 sts rem. Work 3 rows, thus ending with RS facing for next row. Dec 1 st at each end of next and every foll 4th row to 36 sts, then on every foll alt row until 32 sts rem. Dec 1 st at each end of next 5 rows, thus ending with RS facing for next row (22 sts). Cast off 2 sts at beg of next 2 rows. Cast off rem 18 sts.

MAKE UP

Press carefully following instructions on ball band.

Join both shoulder seams.

Button Border

Slip 8 sts left on Left Front safety pin onto 4 mm (USA 6) needles and rejoin yarn with RS facing.

Row 1 - (RS), K1, (K1 tbl) twice, P2, (K1 tbl) twice, K1.

Row 2 - K1, (P1 tbl) twice, K2, (P1 tbl) twice, K1.

Rep last 2 rows until Border, when slightly stretched, fits up Left Front to start of front slope shaping, up front slope and across to centre back neck, sewing in place as you go along and ending with RS facing for next row. Cast off in patt.

Mark positions for 8 buttons on Button Border with pins to ensure even spacing - lowest 3 buttons to be level with buttonholes in right front, top button 1 cm below start of front slope shaping and rem 4 buttons evenly spaced between.

Buttonhole Border

Slip 8 sts left on Right Front safety pin onto 4 mm (USA 6) needles and rejoin yarn with **WS** facing.

Row 1 - (WS), K1, (P1 tbl) twice, K2, (P1 tbl) twice, K1.

Row 2 - K1, (K1 tbl) twice, P2, (K1 tbl) twice, K1.

Rep last 2 rows until Border, when slightly stretched, fits up Right Front to start of front slope shaping, sewing in place as you go along and with the addition of a further 5 buttonholes to correspond with positions marked for buttons.

To make a buttonhole (RS): K1, (K1 tbl) twice, P2tog, (yrn) twice (to make a buttonhole - drop extra loop on next row), (K1 tbl) twice, K1.

Cont in rib, up front slope and across to centre back neck, sewing in place as you go along and ending with RS facing for next row.

Cast off in patt.

Join ends of Borders at centre back neck.

Join side seams. Join sleeve seams.

Insert Sleeves.

Sew on buttons.

51[53.5,55.5,58,60]cm
(20[21,21.75,22.75,23.5]in)

58[58,59,60,60]cm (23[23,23,23.5,23.5]in)

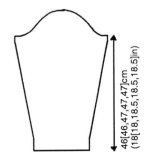

46[46,47,47,47]cm
(18[18,18.5,18.5,18.5]in)

Design 10

Trail

To fit bust

76	**81**	86	**91**	97	**102**	cm
30	**32**	34	**36**	38	**40**	in

Actual size

106	**112**	119	**125**	132	**138**	cm
41½	**44**	47	**49**	52	**54½**	in

Finished length

70	**71**	71	**72**	72	**73**	cm
27½	**28**	28	**28½**	28½	**28½**	in

Sleeve length to underarm

44	**46**	46	**47**	47	**47**	cm
17½	**18**	18	**18½**	18½	**18½**	in

Jaeger Matchmaker Merino Chunky (683)

17	**18**	18	**19**	20	**21**	50 gm

Quantities of yarn are approximate as they are based on average requirements. **Check actual yarn colour - as printing may not match yarn exactly.**

Pair each of 5 mm (UK 6/USA 8) and 5½ mm (UK 5/USA 9) needles. Cable pin.

Tension

15½ sts and 20 rows to 10 cm (stocking st) on 5½ mm (USA 9) needles or size needed to achieve stated tension.

For notes and abbreviations, see page 58.

Special abbreviations

M1P=make a st by picking up horizontal loop lying before next st and purling into back of it.
C4F=slip next 2 sts on cable pin and leave at front of work, K2, then K2 from cable pin.

BACK

With 5 mm (USA 8) needles, cast on 82 [**87**, 92, **97**, 102, **107**] sts.

Cable rib patt thus:

Row 1 - (RS), P2, *K3, P2; rep from * to end.
Row 2 - K2, *P1, M1P (**by picking up horizontal loop lying before next st and purling into back of it**), P2, K2; rep from * to end (98 [**104**, 110, **116**, 122, **128**] sts).
Row 3 - P2, *C4F, P2; rep from * to end.
Row 4 - K2, *P4, K2; rep from * to end.
Row 5 - P2, *K4, P2; rep from * to end.
Rows 6 and 7 - As rows 4 and 5.
Row 8 - As row 4.
Rows 9 to 26 - As rows 3 to 8, 3 times.
Rows 27 and 28 - As rows 3 and 4.
Row 29 - P2, *K1, K2tog, K1, P2; rep from * to end (82 [**87**, 92, **97**, 102, **107**] sts).
Row 30 - K2, *P3, K2; rep from * to end.
Row 31 - As row 1.
Row 32 - As row 30.
Change to 5½ mm (USA 9) needles and starting with a K row, work in stocking st until Back meas 48 cm, ending with RS facing for next row.

Shape armholes

Cast off 5 sts at beg of next 2 rows (72 [**77**, 82, **87**, 92, **97**] sts).
Work straight until armhole meas 22 [**23**, 23, **24**, 24, **25**] cm, end with RS facing for next row.

Shape shoulders and back neck

Cast off 8 [**9**, 9, **10**, 11, **12**] sts at beg of next 2 rows (56 [**59**, 64, **67**, 70, **73**] sts).
Next row - (RS), cast off 8 [**9**, 9, **10**, 11, **12**] sts, K until there are 11 [**11**, 13, **14**, 14, **14**] sts on right needle, turn and work this side first.
Cast off 3 sts at beg of next row. Cast off rem 8 [**8**, 10, **11**, 11, **11**] sts. With RS facing, slip centre 18 [**19**, 20, **19**, 20, **21**] sts onto a spare needle, rejoin yarn to rem sts, K to end. Work to match first side, reversing shapings.

FRONT

Work as Back until 14 rows less have been worked before start of shoulder and back neck shaping, ending with RS facing for next row.

Shape front neck

Next row - (RS), K31 [**33**, 35, **38**, 40, **42**], turn and work this side first.
Cast off 3 sts at beg of next row (28 [**30**, 32, **35**, 37, **39**] sts). Dec 1 st at neck edge on next 2 rows, then on foll 2 alt rows (24 [**26**, 28, **31**, 33, **35**] sts). Work 6 rows, thus ending with RS facing for next row.

Shape shoulder

Cast off 8 [**9**, 9, **10**, 11, **12**] sts at beg of next and foll alt row. Work 1 row.
Cast off rem 8 [**8**, 10, **11**, 11, **11**] sts.
With RS facing, slip centre 10 [**11**, 12, **11**, 12, **13**] sts onto a spare needle, rejoin yarn to rem sts, K to end. Work to match first side, reversing shapings, working an extra row before start of shoulder shaping.

SLEEVES

With 5 mm (USA 8) needles, cast on 42 sts.
Work rows 1 to 20 of cable rib patt as for Back,

noting that there will be 50 sts after row 2. Now work rows 27 to 32 of cable rib patt, **noting** that there will be 42 sts after row 29.
Change to 5½ mm (USA 9) needles and starting with a K row, work in stocking st, shaping sides by inc 1 st at each end of 5th [**5th**, 5th, **5th**, 5th, **3rd**] and every foll 4th [**4th**, 4th, **4th**, 4th, **alt**] row until there are 62 [**70**, 70, **74**, 74, **50**] sts.
76, 81, 86 and 102 cm sizes: Inc 1 st at each end of every foll 6th [**6th**, 6th, **4th**] row from previous inc until there are 68 [**72**, 72, **78**] sts.
All sizes: Work straight until Sleeve meas 44 [**46**, 46, **47**, 47, **47**] cm, ending with RS facing for next row.

Shape top

Place markers at both ends of last row to denote top of sleeve seam.
Work a further 6 rows, thus ending with RS facing for next row. Cast off loosely.

MAKE UP

Press carefully following instructions on ball band.
Join right shoulder seam.

Neck Border

With RS facing and 5 mm (USA 8) needles, **knit up** 21 [**21**, 20, **21**, 20, **20**] sts down left side of front neck, K 10 [**11**, 12, **11**, 12, **13**] sts from front dec 0 [**1**, 0, **1**, 0, **1**] st at centre, **knit up** 21 [**21**, 20, **21**, 20, **20**] sts up right side of front neck, 5 [**5**, 4, **5**, 4, **4**] sts down right side of back neck, K 18 [**19**, 20, **19**, 20, **21**] sts from back dec 0 [**1**, 0, **1**, 0, **1**] st at centre, then knit up 5 [**5**, 4, **5**, 4, **4**] sts up left side of back neck (80 sts).
Row 1 - (WS), K2, *P4, K2; rep from * to end.
Row 2 - P2, *C4F, P2; rep from * to end.
Row 3 - K2, *P4, K2; rep from * to end.
Row 4 - P2, *K4, P2; rep from * to end.
Rows 5 and 6 - As rows 3 and 4.
Rows 7 to 18 - As rows 1 to 6, twice.
Rows 19 and 20 - As rows 1 and 2.
Row 21 - K2, *P1, P2tog, P1, K2; rep from * to end (67 sts).
Row 22 - P2, *K3, P2; rep from * to end.
Cast off loosely in patt.
Join left shoulder seam and Neck Border. Place centre of cast-off edge of Sleeves to shoulder seams, then sew Sleeves into armholes, matching sleeve markers to top of side seams. Join side and sleeve seams.

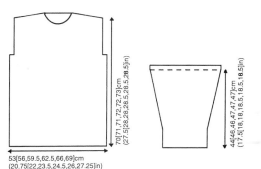

70[71, 71, 72, 72, 73]cm
(27.5[28, 28, 28.5, 28.5, 28.5]in)

44[46, 46, 47, 47, 47]cm
(17.5[18, 18, 18.5, 18.5, 18.5]in)

53[56, 59.5, 62.5, 66, 69]cm
(20.75[22, 23.5, 24.5, 26, 27.25]in)

Design 11

Worth

To fit bust

81	**86**	91	**97**	102	cm
32	**34**	36	**38**	40	in

Actual size

105	**111**	116	**122**	128	cm
41½	**43½**	45½	**48**	50½	in

Finished length

71	**71**	72	**72**	73	cm
28	**28**	28½	**28½**	28½	in

Sleeve length to underarm

46	**46**	47	**47**	47	cm
18	**18**	18½	**18½**	18½	in

Jaeger Matchmaker Merino 4 ply

10	**10**	11	**11**	11	50 gm

Jaeger Cashmere 4 ply (112)

18	**19**	20	**21**	22	25 gm

Jaeger Alpaca 4 ply

10	**10**	11	**11**	11	50 gm

Quantities of yarn are approximate as they are based on average requirements. Check actual yarn colour - as printing may not match yarn exactly.

Matchmaker Merino and Cashmere 4 ply versions: Pair each of 2¾ mm (UK 12/USA 2) and 3¼ mm (UK 10/USA 3) needles.
Alpaca 4 ply version: Pair each of 2¼ mm (UK 13/USA 1) and 3 mm (UK 11/USA 2/3) needles.
All versions: 8 buttons.

Tension

28 sts and 36 rows to 10 cm (patt), 28 sts and 36 rows to 10 cm (stocking st) on larger size needles or size needed to achieve stated tension.

For notes and abbreviations, see page 58.

BACK

With smaller size needles, cast on 147 [**155**, 163, **171**, 179] sts.
Row 1 - (RS), K1, *P1, K1; rep from * to end. This row forms moss st.
Work in moss st for a further 13 rows, thus ending with RS facing for next row.
Change to larger size needles and starting and ending rows at points indicated, work in patt foll chart, repeating the 20 row patt repeat throughout, until Back meas 49 cm, ending with RS facing for next row.
Shape armholes
Keeping patt correct, cast off 7 [**8**, 9, **10**, 11] sts at beg of next 2 rows (133 [**139**, 145, **151**, 157] sts). Dec 1 st at each end of next 3 [**5**, 5, **7**, 7] rows, then on foll 3 [**3**, 4, **4**, 5] alt rows (121 [**123**, 127, **129**, 133] sts). Work 3 rows, thus ending with RS facing for next row. Dec 1 st at each end of next and every foll 4th row until 113 [**115**, 119, **121**, 125] sts rem.
Work straight until armhole meas 22 [**22**, 23, **23**, 24] cm, ending with RS facing for next row.
Shape shoulders and back neck
Cast off 12 [**12**, 12, **13**, 13] sts at beg of next 2 rows (89 [**91**, 95, **95**, 99] sts).
Next row - (RS), cast off 12 [**12**, 12, **13**, 13] sts, patt until there are 15 [**16**, 17, **16**, 17] sts on right needle, turn and work this side first.
Cast off 4 sts at beg of next row.
Cast off rem 11 [**12**, 13, **12**, 13] sts.
With RS facing, rejoin yarn to rem sts, cast off centre 35 [**35**, 37, **37**, 39] sts, patt to end. Work to match first side, reversing shapings.

POCKET LININGS (Make 2)

With larger size needles, cast on 39 sts.
Starting with a K row, work in stocking st for 45 rows, thus ending with **WS** facing for next row.
Break yarn and leave sts on a spare needle.

LEFT FRONT

With smaller size needles, cast on 81 [**85**, 89, **93**, 97] sts.
Work in moss st as on Back for 13 rows, thus ending with **WS** facing for next row.
Next row - (WS), patt 8 sts and slip these 8 sts onto a safety pin for Button Border, M1 (**by picking up horizontal loop lying before next st and working into back of it**), patt to end (74 [**78**, 82, **86**, 90] sts).
Change to larger size needles and starting and ending rows at points indicated, work 45 rows in patt foll chart, repeating the 20 row patt repeat throughout and thus ending with **WS** facing for next row.
Shape pocket front
Next row - (WS), patt 52 and turn, leaving rem 22 [**26**, 30, **34**, 38] sts on a spare needle.
Keeping patt correct, work on this set of 52 sts only for pocket front thus:
Work 2 rows, thus ending with RS facing for next row. Dec 1 st at beg of next and foll 18 alt rows (33 sts).

Work 1 row, ending with RS facing for next row. Break yarn and leave sts on a spare needle.
Shape pocket back
With **WS** facing, rejoin yarn and P 39 sts of first Pocket Lining, then patt rem 22 [**26**, 30, **34**, 38] sts from front (61 [**65**, 69, **73**, 77] sts).
Patt 39 rows, thus ending with **WS** facing for next row. Cast off 20 sts at beg of next row (41 [**45**, 49, **53**, 57] sts).
Join sections
Next row - (RS), patt 41 [**45**, 49, **53**, 57] sts of pocket back, then patt across 33 sts of pocket front (74 [**78**, 82, **86**, 90] sts).
Cont straight until Left Front matches Back to start of armhole shaping, ending with RS facing for next row.
Shape armhole
Keeping patt correct, cast off 7 [**8**, 9, **10**, 11] sts at beg of next row (67 [**70**, 73, **76**, 79] sts).
Work 1 row. Dec 1 st at armhole edge of next 3 [**5**, 5, **7**, 7] rows, then on foll 3 [**3**, 4, **4**, 5] alt rows (61 [**62**, 64, **65**, 67] sts). Work 3 rows, thus ending with RS facing for next row. Dec 1 st at armhole edge of next and every foll 4th row until 57 [**58**, 60, **61**, 63] sts rem.
Work straight until 23 rows less have been worked than on Back to start of shoulder shaping, ending with **WS** facing for next row.
Shape neck
Keeping patt correct, cast off 10 [**10**, 11, **11**, 12] sts at beg of next row, then 4 sts at beg of foll alt row (43 [**44**, 45, **46**, 47] sts). Dec 1 st at neck edge of next 4 rows, then on foll 2 alt rows (37 [**38**, 39, **40**, 41] sts). Work 3 rows.
Dec 1 st at neck edge of next and foll 4th row (35 [**36**, 37, **38**, 39] sts). Work 4 rows, thus ending with RS facing for next row.
Shape shoulders and back neck
Cast off 12 [**12**, 12, **13**, 13] sts at beg of next and foll alt row. Work 1 row.
Cast off rem 11 [**12**, 13, **12**, 13] sts.

RIGHT FRONT

With smaller size needles, cast on 81 [**85**, 89, **93**, 97] sts.
Work in moss st as on Back for 6 rows, thus ending with RS facing for next row.
Next row - (RS), patt 3 sts, (yrn) twice (to make a buttonhole - drop extra loop on next row), work 2 tog, patt to end.
Work in moss st for a further 6 rows, thus ending with **WS** facing for next row.
Next row - (WS), patt to last 8 sts, M1, turn and slip last 8 sts onto a safety pin for Buttonhole Border (74 [**78**, 82, **86**, 90] sts).
Change to larger size needles and starting and ending rows at points indicated, work 45 rows in patt foll chart, repeating the 20 row patt repeat throughout and thus ending with **WS** facing for next row.
Shape pocket back
Next row - (WS), patt 22 [**26**, 30, **34**, 38] sts, slip rem 52 sts onto a spare needle for pocket front and, in their place, P across 39 sts of

second Pocket Lining (61 [**65**, 69, **73**, 77] sts).
Patt 39 rows, end with **WS** facing for next row.
Next row - (**WS**), patt to last 20 sts, cast off
last 20 sts.
Break yarn and leave rem 41 [**45**, 49, **53**, 57]
sts on a spare needle.

Shape pocket front
With **WS** facing, rejoin yarn to rem 52 sts and
patt 3 rows, thus ending with RS facing for next
row. Dec 1 st at end of next and foll 18 alt rows
(33 sts). Work 1 row, thus ending with RS
facing for next row.

Join sections
Next row - (**RS**), patt 33 sts of pocket front,
then patt across 41 [**45**, 49, **53**, 57] sts of
pocket back (74 [**78**, 82, **86**, 90] sts).
Complete to match Left Front, reversing
shapings, working an extra row before start of
armhole, neck and shoulder shaping.

SLEEVES
With smaller size needles, cast on 71 sts.
Work in moss st as on Back for 14 rows, thus
ending with RS facing for next row.
Change to larger size needles and starting
and ending rows at points indicated, work in
patt foll chart, repeating the 20 row patt repeat
throughout, shaping sides by inc 1 st at each
end of chart row 1 and every foll 8th [**8th**, 6th,
6th, 6th] row to 77 [**97**, 77, **93**, 109] sts, then
on every foll 10th [**10th**, 8th, **8th**, 8th] row until
there are 101 [**105**, 109, **113**, 117] sts, taking
inc sts into patt.
Work straight until Sleeve meas 46 [**46**, 47, **47**,
47] cm, ending with RS facing for next row.

Shape top
Keeping patt correct, cast off 7 [**8**, 9, **10**, 11]
sts at beg of next 2 rows (87 [**89**, 91, **93**, 95]
sts). Dec 1 st at each end of next 5 rows, then
on foll 6 alt rows (65 [**67**, 69, **71**, 73] sts). Work
3 rows, thus ending with RS facing for next row.
Dec 1 st at each end of next and every foll 4th
row until 57 [**61**, 61, **65**, 65] sts rem, then on
foll 4 [**6**, 6, **8**, 8] alt rows, thus ending with **WS**
facing for next row (49 sts). Dec 1 st at each
end of next 7 rows (35 sts). Cast off 4 sts at
beg of next 4 rows. Cast off rem 19 sts.

MAKE UP
Press carefully following instructions on ball
band.
Join both shoulder seams.

Button Border
Slip 8 sts left on Left Front safety pin onto
smaller size needles and rejoin yarn with RS
facing.
Cont in moss st as set until Border, when
slightly stretched, fits up left front opening
edge to neck shaping, sewing in place as you
go along and ending with RS facing for next
row. Cast off in patt.
Mark positions for 8 buttons on this Border with
pins to ensure even spacing - lowest button to
be level with buttonhole already worked in

Right Front, top button 1.5 cm below neck
shaping and rem 6 buttons evenly spaced
between.

Buttonhole Border
Slip 8 sts left on Right Front safety pin onto
smaller size needles and rejoin yarn with **WS**
facing. Cont in moss st as set until Border,
when slightly stretched, fits up right front
opening edge to start of neck shaping, with the
addition of a further 7 buttonholes to
correspond with positions marked for buttons,
sewing in place as you go along and ending
with RS facing for next row. Cast off in patt.
To make a buttonhole: (RS), patt 3 sts, (yrn)
twice (to make a buttonhole - drop extra loop
on next row), work 2 tog, patt 3 sts.

Collar
With smaller size needles, cast on 121 [**121**,
125, **125**, 129] sts.
Row 1 - (RS), K3, *P1, K1; rep from * to last
4 sts, P1, K3.
This row sets position of moss st, with edge
3 sts worked as K sts on every row.
Keeping patt correct, work a further 11 rows,
thus ending with RS facing for next row.
Next row - K3, M1, patt to last 3 sts, M1, K3.
Work 2 rows.
Rep last 3 rows until Collar meas 7.5 cm.
Cast off in patt.
Positioning row ends of collar midway across
top of Borders, sew cast-on edge of Collar to
neck edge.

Pocket Tops
With RS facing and smaller size needles, knit
up 37 sts along sloping pocket opening edge.
Work in moss st as on Back for 6 rows.
Cast off in patt.
Sew Pocket Linings in place on inside and sew
down ends of Pocket Tops.
Join side seams. Join sleeve seams.
Insert Sleeves.
Sew on buttons.

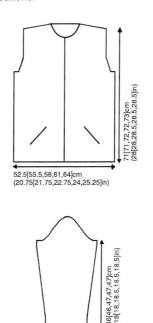

52.5[55.5,58,61,64]cm
(20.75[21.75,22.75,24,25.25]in)

71[71,72,72,73]cm
(28[28,28.5,28.5,28.5]in)

46[46,47,47,47]cm
(18[18,18.5,18.5,18.5]in)

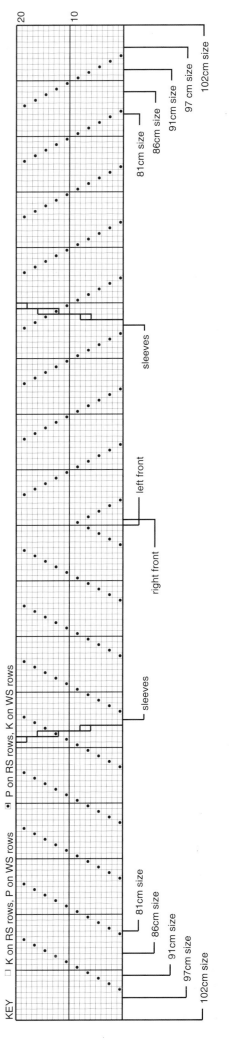

KEY
□ K on RS rows, P on WS rows
▣ P on RS rows, K on WS rows

81cm size
86cm size
91cm size
97 cm size
102cm size

sleeves
left front
right front
sleeves

Design 12

Clover

To fit chest/bust

61	**66**	71	**76**	81	**86**	91	**97**	102	cm
24	**26**	28	**30**	32	**34**	36	**38**	40	in

Actual size, at underarm

75	**83**	90	**97**	105	**112**	119	**126**	134	cm
29½	**32½**	35½	**38**	41½	**44**	47	**49½**	53	in

Finished length

40	**44**	48	**51**	56	**61**	62	**63**	64	cm
15½	**17½**	19	**20**	22	**24**	24½	**25**	25	in

Sleeve length to underarm

30	**34**	38	**42**	46	**46**	47	**47**	47	cm
12	**13½**	15	**16½**	18	**18**	18½	**18½**	18½	in

Jaeger Matchmaker Merino DK (639 or 863)

6	**7**	8	**9**	10	**11**	12	**13**	14	50 g

Jaeger Extra Fine Merino DK

6	**7**	8	**9**	10	**11**	12	**13**	13	50 g

Quantities of yarn are approximate as they are based on average requirements.

Check actual yarn colour - as printing may not match yarn exactly.

Matchmaker Merino DK version: Pair each of 3¼ mm (UK 10/USA 3) and 4 mm (UK 8/USA 6) needles.
Extra Fine Merino DK version: Pair each of 3 mm (UK 11/USA 2/3) and 3¾ mm (UK 9/USA 5) needles.
Both versions: One 50 gram ball of same yarn in contrast colour for embroidery.
5 [**5**, 5, **5**, 6, **6**, 6, **6**, 6] buttons.

Tension
Matchmaker Merino DK version: 22 sts and 30 rows to 10 cm (stocking st) on 4 mm (USA 6) needles or size needed to achieve stated tension.

Extra Fine Merino DK version: 22 sts and 32 rows to 10 cm (stocking st) on 3¾ mm (USA 5) needles or size needed to achieve stated tension.

For notes and abbreviations, see page 58.

BACK

With smaller size needles, cast on 77 [**85**, 93, **101**, 105, **113**, 121, **129**, 137] sts.
Row 1 - (RS), K1, *P1, K1; rep from * to end.
This row forms moss st.
Work in moss st for a further 9 rows, thus ending with RS facing for next row.
Change to larger size needles and starting with a K row, work in stocking st for 2 rows. Starting and ending rows as indicated and repeating the 8 patt sts 8 [**10**, 10, **12**, 12, **14**, 14, **16**, 16] times across each row, now work foll chart A until chart row 10 is completed, thus ending with RS facing for next row.
Next row - (RS), K3, M1 (**by picking up horizontal loop lying before next st and working into back of it**), K to last 3 sts, M1, K3.
(79[**87**, 95, **103**, 107, **115**, 123, **131**, 139] sts).
Working all increases (on Back, Fronts and Sleeves) as set by last row and starting with a P row, cont in stocking st, shaping sides by inc 1 st at each end of every foll 16th [**16th**, 18th, **20th**, 16th, **18th**, 18th, **18th**, 18th] row from previous inc until there are 83 [**91**, 99, **107**, 115, **123**, 131, **139**, 147] sts.
Work straight until Back meas 22 [**25**, 28, **30**, 34, **38**, 38, **39**, 39] cm, ending with RS facing for next row.
Shape armholes
Cast off 4 [**4**, 4, **4**, 5, **5**, 5, **5**, 5] sts at beg of next 2 rows (75 [**83**, 91, **99**, 105, **113**, 121, **129**, 137] sts). Dec 1 st at each end of next and foll 4 [**4**, 4, **4**, 7, **7**, 7, **7**, 7] rows (65 [**73**, 81, **89**, 89, **97**, 105, **113**, 121] sts).
Work straight until armhole meas 18 [**19**, 20, **21**, 22, **23**, 24, **24**, 25] cm, ending with RS facing for next row.
Shape shoulders and back neck
Cast off 6 [**7**, 8, **10**, 9, **10**, 12, **13**, 14] sts at beg of next 2 rows
(53 [**59**, 65, **69**, 71, **77**, 81, **87**, 93] sts).
Next row - (RS), cast off 6 [**7**, 8, **10**, 9, **10**, 12, **13**, 14] sts, K until there are 11 [**12**, 13, **13**, 14, **15**, 15, **16**, 18] sts on right needle, turn and work this side first.
Cast off 4 sts at beg of next row.
Cast off rem 7 [**8**, 9, **9**, 10, **11**, 11, **12**, 14] sts.
With RS facing, rejoin yarn to rem sts, cast off centre 19 [**21**, 23, **23**, 25, **27**, 27, **29**, 29] sts, K to end. Work to match first side, reversing shapings.

LEFT FRONT

With smaller size needles, cast on 41 [**45**, 49, **53**, 55, **59**, 63, **67**, 71] sts.
Work in moss st as for Back for 9 rows, thus ending with **WS** facing for next row.

Next row - (WS), patt 6 sts and slip these sts onto a safety pin for Button Border, M1, patt to end (36 [**40**, 44, **48**, 50, **54**, 58, **62**, 66] sts).
Change to larger size needles and starting with a K row, work in stocking st for 2 rows. Starting and ending rows as indicated and repeating the 8 patt sts 3 [**3**, 4, **4**, 5, **5**, 6, **6**, 7] times across each row, now work foll chart B until chart row 18 is completed, inc 1 st (in same way as on Back) at beg of chart row 11 and thus ending with RS facing for next row (37 [**41**, 45, **49**, 51, **55**, 59, **63**, 67] sts).
Now repeating chart rows 11 to 18 **only**, cont in patt, shaping sides by inc 1 st at beg of every foll 16th [**16th**, 18th, **20th**, 16th, **18th**, 18th, **18th**, 18th] row from previous inc until there are 39 [**43**, 47, **51**, 55, **59**, 63, **67**, 71] sts.
Work straight until Left Front matches Back to start of armhole shaping, ending with RS facing for next row.
Shape armholes
Keeping patt correct, cast off 4 [**4**, 4, **4**, 5, **5**, 5, **5**, 5] sts at beg of next row (35 [**39**, 43, **47**, 50, **54**, 58, **62**, 66] sts). Work 1 row. Dec 1 st at armhole edge of next and foll 4 [**4**, 4, **4**, 7, **7**, 7, **7**, 7] rows (30 [**34**, 38, **42**, 42, **46**, 50, **54**, 58] sts).
Work straight until 13 [**15**, 15, **17**, 17, **19**, 19, **21**, 21] rows less have been worked than on Back to start of shoulder shaping, ending with **WS** facing for next row.
Shape neck
Cast off 5 [**6**, 7, **7**, 7, **8**, 8, **9**, 9] sts at beg of next row (25 [**28**, 31, **35**, 35, **38**, 42, **45**, 49] sts).
Dec 1 st at neck edge on next 4 rows, then on foll 2 alt rows
(19 [**22**, 25, **29**, 29, **32**, 36, **39**, 43] sts).
81, 86, 91, 97 and 102 cm sizes:
Work 3 rows.
Dec 1 st at neck edge on next row
([**28**, **31**, 35, **38**, 42] sts).
All sizes: Work 4 [**6**, 6, **8**, 4, **6**, 6, **8**, 8] rows, thus ending with RS facing for next row.
Shape shoulder
Cast off 6 [**7**, 8, **10**, 9, **10**, 12, **13**, 14] sts at beg of next and foll alt row.
Work 1 row.
Cast off rem 7 [**8**, 9, **9**, 10, **11**, 11, **12**, 14] sts.

RIGHT FRONT

With smaller size needles, cast on 41 [**45**, 49, **53**, 55, **59**, 63, **67**, 71] sts.
Work in moss st as for Back for 4 rows.
Next row - (RS), K1, P1, K2tog, (yrn) twice (to make a buttonhole - drop extra loop on next row), patt to end.
Work in moss st for a further 4 rows, thus ending with **WS** facing for next row.
Next row - (WS), patt to last 6 sts, M1, turn and slip last 6 sts onto a safety pin for Buttonhole Border
(36 [**40**, 44, **48**, 50, **54**, 58, **62**, 66] sts).
Change to larger size needles and starting with a K row, work in stocking st for 2 rows.

44

Starting and ending rows as indicated and repeating the 8 patt sts 3 [3, 4, 4, 5, **5**, 6, **6**, 7] times across each row, now work foll chart C until chart row 18 is completed, inc 1 st (in same way as on Back) at end of chart row 11 and thus ending with RS facing for next row (37 [**41**, 45, **49**, 51, **55**, 59, **63**, 67] sts). Complete to match Left Front, reversing shapings, working an extra row before start of armhole, neck and shoulder shapings.

SLEEVES

With smaller size needles, cast on 45 [**45**, 47, **51**, 55, **59**, 59, **61**, 61] sts.

Work in moss st as for Back for 10 rows, thus ending with RS facing for next row.

Change to larger size needles and starting with a K row, work in stocking st for 2 rows, inc 1 st at each end of first of these rows (47 [**47**, 49, **53**, 57, **61**, 61, **63**, 63] sts). Starting and ending rows as indicated and repeating the 8 patt sts 5 [**5**, 5, **5**, 5, **7**, 7, **7**, 7] times across each row, now work foll chart D until chart row 10 is completed, inc 1 st at each end of chart row 3 and every foll 4th [**4th**, 4th, **4th**, 6th, **6th**, 4th, **4th**, 4th] row and thus ending with RS facing for next row (51 [**51**, 53, **57**, 61, **65**, 65, **67**, 67] sts). Working all increases as set by Back and starting with a K row, cont in stocking st, shaping sides by inc 1 st at each end of every foll 4th [**4th**, 4th, **4th**, 6th, **6th**, 4th, **4th**, 4th] row from previous inc until there are 79 [**79**, 75, **67**, 97, **101**, 73, **69**, 81] sts.

61, 66, 71, 76, 91, 97 and 102 cm sizes: Inc 1 st at each end of every foll 6th row from previous inc until there are 81 [**85**, 89, **93**, 105, **105**, 109] sts.

All sizes: Work straight until Sleeve meas 30 [**34**, 38, **42**, 46, **46**, 47, **47**, 47] cm, ending with RS facing for next row.

Shape top

Cast off 4 [**4**, 4, **4**, 5, **5**, 5, **5**, 5] sts at beg of next 2 rows (73 [**77**, 81, **85**, 87, **91**, 95, **95**, 99] sts). Dec 1 st at each end of next and foll 3 [**3**, 3, **3**, 6, **6**, 6, **6**, 6] alt rows (65 [**69**, 73, **77**, 73, **77**, 81, **81**, 85] sts). Dec 1 st at each end of next row, thus ending with RS facing for next row. Cast off rem 63 [**67**, 71, **75**, 71, **75**, 79, **79**, 83] sts loosely.

MAKE UP

Press carefully following instructions on ball band.

Join both shoulder seams.

Button Border

Slip 6 sts left on Left Front safety pin onto smaller size needles and rejoin yarn with RS facing.

Cont in moss st as set until Border, when slightly stretched, fits up left front opening edge to neck shaping, sewing in place as you go along and ending with RS facing for next row. Cast off in patt.

Mark positions for 5 [**5**, 5, **5**, 6, **6**, 6, **6**, 6] buttons on this Border with pins to ensure even spacing - lowest button level with buttonhole already worked in Right Front, top button 1.5 cm below neck shaping and rem 3 [**3**, 3, **3**, 4, **4**, 4, **4**, 4] buttons evenly spaced between.

Buttonhole Border

Slip 6 sts left on Right Front safety pin onto smaller size needles and rejoin yarn with **WS** facing.

Cont in moss st as set until Border, when slightly stretched, fits up right front opening edge to neck shaping, with the addition of a further 4 [**4**, 4, **4**, 5, **5**, 5, **5**, 5] buttonholes to correspond with positions marked for buttons, sewing in place as you go along and ending with RS facing for next row. Cast off in patt.

To make a buttonhole: (RS), K1, P1, K2tog, (yrn) twice (to make a buttonhole - drop extra loop on next row), K1, P1.

Collar

With smaller size needles, cast on 81 [**85**, 87, **89**, 93, **97**, 97, **101**, 101] sts.

Row 1 - (RS), K3, *P1, K1; rep from * to last 4 sts, P1, K3.

This row sets position of moss st, with edge 3 sts worked as K sts on every row.

Keeping patt correct, work a further 9 rows, thus ending with RS facing for next row.

Next row - K3, M1, patt to last 3 sts, M1, K3. Work 2 rows.

Rep last 3 rows until Collar meas 7 [**7**, 7, **7**, 8, **8**, 8, **8**, 8] cm. Cast off in patt.

Positioning row ends of Collar midway across top of Borders, sew cast-on edge of Collar to neck edge.

Place centre of cast-off edge of Sleeves to shoulder seams, then sew Sleeves into armholes, matching shaped edges. Join side and sleeve seams. Sew on buttons.

Embroidery: With contrast colour yarn, embroider a flower (made up of 4 lazy daisy stitches radiating out from centre) inside each complete diamond around lower and cuff edges and up fronts.

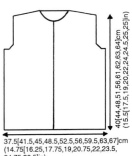

40[44,48,51,56,61,62,63,64]cm
(15.5[17.5,19,20,22,24,24.5,25,25]in)

37.5[41.5,45,48.5,52.5,56,59.5,63,67]cm
(14.75[16.25,17.75,19,20.75,22,23.5, 24.75,26.5]in)

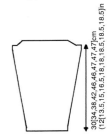

30[34,38,42,46,46,47,47,47]cm
(12[13.5,15,16.5,18,18,18.5,18.5,18.5]in)

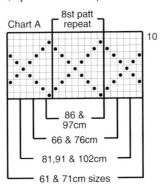

Chart A — 8st patt repeat — 10

86 & 97cm
66 & 76cm
81,91 & 102cm
61 & 71cm sizes

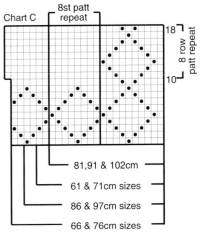

Chart C — 8st patt repeat — 18 — 8 row patt repeat — 10

81,91 & 102cm
61 & 71cm sizes
86 & 97cm sizes
66 & 76cm sizes

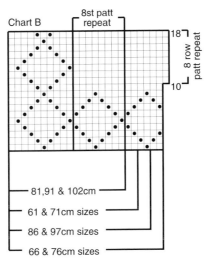

Chart B — 8st patt repeat — 18 — 8 row patt repeat — 10

81,91 & 102cm
61 & 71cm sizes
86 & 97cm sizes
66 & 76cm sizes

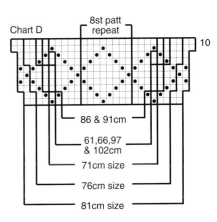

Chart D — 8st patt repeat — 10

86 & 91cm
61,66,97 & 102cm
71cm size
76cm size
81cm size

Key ▢ K on RS rows, P on WS rows   ● P on RS rows, K on WS rows

Design 13

Mischief

To fit bust

81	86	91	97	102	cm
32	34	36	38	40	in

Actual size

111	116	120	124	129	cm
43½	45½	47	49	51	in

Finished length

71	71	72	72	73	cm
28	28	28½	28½	28½	in

Sleeve length to underarm

46	46	47	47	47	cm
18	18	18½	18½	18½	in

Jaeger Matchmaker Merino DK (865)

17	17	18	19	19	50 gm

Jaeger Extra Fine Merino DK

16	17	18	18	19	50 gm

Quantities of yarn are approximate as they are based on average requirements.

Check actual yarn colour - as printing may not match yarn exactly.

Matchmaker Merino DK version: Pair each of 3¼ mm (UK 10/USA 3) and 4 mm (UK 8/USA 6) needles.
Extra Fine Merino DK version: Pair each of 3 mm (UK 11/USA 2/3) and 3¾ mm (UK 9/USA 5) needles.

Both versions: Cable pin.

Tension
Matchmaker Merino DK version: 28 sts and 30 rows to 10 cm (patt), 22 sts and 30 rows to 10 cm (stocking st) on 4 mm (USA 6) needles or size needed to achieve stated tension.

Extra Fine Merino DK version: 28 sts and 32 rows to 10 cm (patt), 22 sts and 32 rows to 10 cm (stocking st) on 3¾ mm (USA 5) needles or size needed to achieve stated tension.

For notes and abbreviations, see page 58.

Special note
When casting off, dec 2 sts across top of each cable. St counts given are prior to these decreases.

Special abbreviations
C4F=slip next 2 sts on cable pin and leave at front of work, K2, then K2 from cable pin.
C6F=slip next 3 sts on cable pin and leave at front of work, K3, then K3 from cable pin.
Cr3L=slip next 2 sts on cable pin and leave at front of work, P1, then K2 from cable pin.
Cr3R=slip next st on cable pin and leave at back of work, K2, then P1 from cable pin.
Cr5L=slip next 3 sts on cable pin and leave at front of work, P2, then K3 from cable pin.
Cr5R=slip next 2 sts on cable pin and leave at back of work, K3, then P2 from cable pin.
MB=make bobble as follows: K into front, back and then front again of next st, (turn, K3) 3 times, turn, sL1K, K2tog, psso.

BACK
With smaller size needles, cast on 128 [**132**, 138, **144**, 150] sts.
Row 1 - (RS), P0 [**0**, 0, **0**, 3], K0 [**0**, 0, **4**, 4], P0 [**2**, 5, **4**, 4], *K2, P4, K4, P4; rep from * to last 2 [**4**, 7, **10**, 13] sts, K2, P0 [**2**, 5, **4**, 4], K0 [**0**, 0, **4**, 4], P0 [**0**, 0, **0**, 3].
Row 2 and every foll alt row - K0 [**0**, 0, **0**, 3], P0 [**0**, 0, **4**, 4], K0 [**2**, 5, **4**, 4], *P2, K4, P4, K4; rep from * to last 2 [**4**, 7, **10**, 13] sts, P2, K0 [**2**, 5, **4**, 4], P0 [**0**, 0, **4**, 4], K0 [**0**, 0, **0**, 3].
Row 3 - P0 [**0**, 0, **0**, 3], K0 [**0**, 0, **4**, 0], (C4F) 0 [**0**, 0, **0**, 1] time, P0 [**2**, 5, **4**, 4], *K2, P4, C4F, P4; rep from * to last 2 [**4**, 7, **10**, 13] sts, K2, P0 [**2**, 5, **4**, 4], (C4F) 0 [**0**, 0, **0**, 1] time, K0 [**0**, 0, **4**, 0], P0 [**0**, 0, **0**, 3].
Row 5 - As row 1.
Row 6 - As row 2.
Rep last 6 rows 3 times more, and then row 1 again, thus ending with **WS** facing for next row.
Increase row - K0 [**0**, 0, **0**, 3], P0 [**0**, 0, **4**, 4], K0 [**2**, 5, **4**, 4], (M1 **by picking up horizontal loop lying before next st and working into back of it**) 0 [**1**, 1, **1**, 1] time, *P2, M1, K4, M1, P4, M1, K4, M1, P2, M1, K4, P4, K4, M1; rep from * to last 16 [**18**, 21, **24**, 27] sts, P2, M1, K4, M1, P4, M1, K4, M1, P2, (M1) 0 [**1**, 1, **1**, 1] time, K0 [**2**, 5, **4**, 4], P0 [**0**, 0, **4**, 4], K0 [**0**, 0, **0**, 3] (156 [**162**, 168, **174**, 180] sts).
Change to larger size needles and patt thus:
Row 1 - (RS), P3 [**6**, 9, **12**, 15], work next 150 sts as row 1 of chart, P3 [**6**, 9, **12**, 15].
Row 2 - K3 [**6**, 9, **12**, 15], work next 150 sts as row 2 of chart, K3 [**6**, 9, **12**, 15].

These 2 rows set position of chart with edge sts worked in reverse stocking st.
81 and 86 cm sizes: Cont in patt, **repeating chart rows 1 to 12 only**, until Back meas approx 46 cm, ending after chart row 12 and thus with RS facing for next row.
Now cont in patt following chart, **repeating chart rows 13 to 24 only**, until Back meas 48 cm, ending with RS facing for next row.
Shape armholes
Keeping patt correct, cast off 6 [**8**] sts at beg of next 2 rows (144 [**146**] sts).
Work straight, **repeating chart rows 13 to 24 only**, until armhole meas 23 cm, ending with RS facing for next row.
91, 97 and 102 cm sizes: Cont in patt, **repeating chart rows 1 to 12 only**, until Back meas 48 cm, end with RS facing for next row.
Shape armholes
Keeping patt correct, cast off 8 sts at beg of next 2 rows ([152, **158**, 164] sts).
Work straight, **still repeating chart rows 1 to 12 only**, until armhole meas [24, **24**, 25] cm, ending with RS facing for next row.
All sizes
Shape shoulders and back neck
Keeping patt correct and decreasing sts as required (see special note), cast off 16 [**16**, 17, **18**, 19] sts at beg of next 2 rows (112 [**114**, 118, **122**, 126] sts).
Next row - (RS), cast off 16 [**16**, 17, **18**, 19] sts, patt until there are 20 [**21**, 22, **23**, 24] sts on right needle, turn and work this side first.
Cast off 4 sts at beg of next row.
Cast off rem 16 [**17**, 18, **19**, 20] sts.
With RS facing, slip centre 40 sts onto a spare needle, rejoin yarn to rem sts, patt to end.
Work to match first side, reversing shapings.

FRONT
Work as Back until 24 rows less have been worked before start of shoulder and back neck shaping, ending with RS facing for next row.
Shape front neck
Next row - (RS), patt 60 [**61**, 64, **67**, 70], turn and work this side first.
Cast off 4 sts at beg of next row (56 [**57**, 60, **63**, 66] sts). Dec 1 st at neck edge on next 4 rows, then on foll 2 alt rows (50 [**51**, 54, **57**, 60] sts). Work 3 rows. Dec 1 st at neck edge on next and foll 4th row (48 [**49**, 52, **55**, 58] sts). Work 6 rows, end with RS facing for next row.

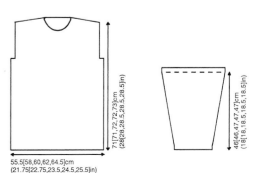

55.5[58,60,62,64.5]cm
(21.75[22.75,23.5,24.5,25.5]in)

71[71,72,72,73]cm
(28[28,28.5,28.5,28.5]in)

46[46,47,47,47]cm
(18[18,18.5,18.5,18.5]in)

Shape shoulder

Keeping patt correct and decreasing sts as required (see special note), cast off 16 [**16**, 17, **18**, 19] sts at beg of next and foll alt row. Work 1 row. Cast off rem 16 [**17**, 18, **19**, 20] sts. With RS facing, slip centre 24 sts onto a spare needle, rejoin yarn to rem sts, patt to end. Work to match first side, rev shapings, working an extra row before start of shoulder shaping.

SLEEVES

With smaller size needles, cast on 64 sts.
Row 1 - (RS), P2, *K4, P4, K2, P4; rep from * to last 6 sts, K4, P2.
Row 2 and every foll alt row - K2, *P4, K4, P2, K4; rep from * to last 6 sts, P4, K2.
Row 3 - P2, *C4F, P4, K2, P4; rep from * to last 6 sts, C4F, P2.
Row 5 - As row 1.
Row 6 - As row 2.
Rep last 6 rows 3 times more, and then row 1 again, thus ending with **WS** facing for next row.
Increase row - K2, M1, *P4, M1, K4, M1, P2, M1, K4, P4, K4, M1, P2, M1, K4, M1; rep from * to last 6 sts, P4, M1, K2 (78 sts).
Change to larger size needles and starting with chart row 1, work in patt foll chart, **repeating chart rows 1 to 24 throughout** and shaping sides by inc 1 st at each end of chart row 1 and every foll 4th [**4th**, alt, **alt**, alt] row to 124 [**124**, 88, **88**, 100] sts, then on every foll 6th [**6th**, 4th, **4th**, 4th] row from previous inc until there are 128 [**128**, 134, **134**, 140] sts, taking inc sts into patt.
All sizes: Work straight until Sleeve meas 46 [**46**, 47, **47**, 47] cm, ending with RS facing for next row.

Shape top

Place markers at both ends of last row to denote top of sleeve seam. Cont straight until Sleeve meas 48 [**49**, 50, **50**, 50] cm, ending with RS facing for next row. Decreasing sts as required (see special note), cast off in patt.

MAKE UP

Press carefully following instructions on ball band.
Join right shoulder seam.

Neck Border

With RS facing and smaller needles, **knit up** 28 sts down left front neck, patt 24 sts from front, **knit up** 28 sts up right front neck, 4 sts down right back neck, patt 40 sts from back as follows: P1, *(K2tog) twice, patt 13; rep from * once more, (K2tog) twice, P1, then **knit up** 4 sts up left back neck (122 sts).
Row 1 and every foll alt row - (**WS**), P2, K4, (P2, K4, P4, K4) twice, (P2, K4) 3 times, (P4, K4, P2, K4) 5 times.
Row 2 - (P4, K2, P4, C4F) 5 times, (P4, K2) 3 times, (P4, C4F, P4, K2) twice, P4, K2.
Row 4 - (P4, K2, P4, K4) 5 times, (P4, K2) 3 times, (P4, K4, P4, K2) twice, P4, K2.
Row 6 - As row 4.

Rep last 6 rows 3 times more, and then rows 1 to 3 again. Decreasing sts as required (see special note), cast off loosely and evenly in patt. Join left shoulder seam and Neck Border. Place centre of cast-off edge of Sleeves to shoulder seams, then sew Sleeves into armholes, matching sleeve markers to top of side seams. Join side and sleeve seams.

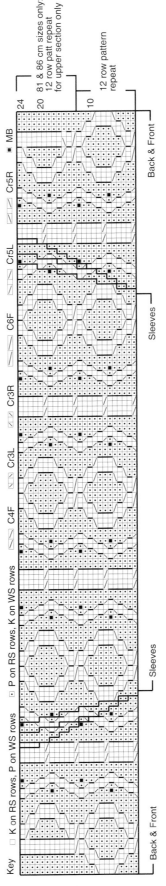

Design 14

Voyage

To fit bust			
76-81	**86-91**	97-102	cm
30-32	**34-36**	38-40	in

Actual size, at underarm
120	**129**	138	cm
47	**51**	54½	in

Finished length
91	**92**	93	cm
36	**36**	36½	in

Sleeve length to underarm, with cuff turned back
46	**47**	47	cm
18	**18½**	18½	in

Jaeger Matchmaker Merino Chunky (404)
28	**30**	32	50 gm

Quantities of yarn are approximate as they are based on average requirements. Check actual yarn colour - as printing may not match yarn exactly.

Pair each of 5 mm (UK 6/USA 8) and 5½ mm (UK 5/USA 9) needles.

Tension
15½ sts and 20 rows to 10 cm (stocking st), 18 sts and 20 rows to 10 cm (rib patt after pressing) on 5½ mm (USA 9) needles or size needed to achieve stated tension.

For notes and abbreviations, see page 58.

BACK

With 5 mm (USA 8) needles, cast on 100 [**108**, 116] sts.
Rib patt thus:
Row 1 - (RS), P4 [**0**, 4], *(K1 tbl) 4 times, P4; rep from * to last 0 [**4**, 0] sts, (K1 tbl) 0 [**4**, 0] times.

Row 2 - K4 [**0**, 4], *(P1 tbl) 4 times, K4; rep from * to last 0 [**4**, 0] sts, (P1 tbl) 0 [**4**, 0] times.
These 2 rows form rib patt.
Patt a further 8 rows, thus ending with RS facing for next row.
Change to 5½ mm (USA 9) needles and work in rib patt for a further 20 rows, thus ending with RS facing for next row.
Shape side seams
Cont in rib patt, shaping side seams by inc 1 st at each end of next and every foll 20th row until there are 108 [**116**, 124] sts, taking inc sts into patt.
Work straight until Back meas 64 cm, ending with RS facing for next row.
Shape armholes
Keeping patt correct, cast off 4 sts at beg of next 2 rows (100 [**108**, 116] sts).
Dec 1 st at each end of next and foll 5 alt rows (88 [**96**, 104] sts).
Work straight until armhole meas 27 [**28**, 29] cm, ending with RS facing for next row.
Shape shoulders and back neck
Keeping patt correct, cast off 10 [**12**, 13] sts at beg of next 2 rows (68 [**72**, 78] sts).
Next row - (RS), cast off 10 [**12**, 13] sts, patt until there are 14 [**14**, 16] sts on right needle, turn and work this side first.
Cast off 3 sts at beg of next row.
Cast off rem 11 [**11**, 13] sts.
With RS facing, rejoin yarn to rem sts, cast off centre 20 sts, patt to end.
Work to match first side, reversing shapings.

POCKET LININGS (Make 2)

With 5½ mm (USA 9) needles cast on 28 sts.
Row 1 - (RS), P4, *(K1 tbl) 4 times, P4; rep from * to end.
Row 2 - K4, *(P1 tbl) 4 times, K4; rep from * to end.
Rep last 2 rows 14 times more, thus ending with RS facing for next row.
Break yarn and leave sts on a spare needle.

LEFT FRONT

With 5 mm (USA 8) needles, cast on 46 [**50**, 54] sts.
Rib patt thus:
Row 1 - (RS), P4 [**0**, 4], *(K1 tbl) 4 times, P4; rep from * to last 10 sts, (K1 tbl) 10 times.
Row 2 - (P1 tbl) 10 times, *K4, (P1 tbl) 4 times; rep from * to last 4 [**0**, 4] sts, K4 [**0**, 4].
These 2 rows form rib patt.
Patt a further 8 rows, thus ending with RS facing for next row.
Change to 5½ mm (USA 9) needles and work in rib patt for a further 20 rows, thus ending with RS facing for next row.
Shape side seam
Cont in rib patt, shaping side seams by inc 1 st at beg of next and foll 20th row, taking inc sts into patt (48 [**52**, 56] sts).
Patt 19 rows, thus ending with RS facing for next row.

Place pocket
Next row - (RS), inc in first st, patt 9 [**13**, 17], slip next 28 sts onto a spare needle and, in their place, patt across 28 sts of first Pocket Lining, patt 10 (49 [**53**, 57] sts).
Patt 19 rows, thus ending with RS facing for next row.
Inc 1 st at beg of next row (50 [**54**, 58] sts).
Work straight until 8 rows less have been worked than on Back to start of armhole shaping, ending with RS facing for next row.
Shape front slope
Next row - (RS), patt to last 5 sts, sL1K, K1, psso, (K1 tbl) 3 times (49 [**53**, 57] sts).
Working all front slope decreases as set by last row, proceed thus:
Patt 7 rows, dec 1 st at front slope edge on 6th of these rows and thus ending with RS facing for next row (48 [**52**, 56] sts).
Shape armhole
Keeping patt correct, cast off 4 sts at beg of next row (44 [**48**, 52] sts). Work 1 row.
Dec 1 st at armhole edge of next and foll 5 alt rows **and at same time** dec 1 st at front slope edge on every foll 6th row from previous dec (36 [**40**, 44] sts).
Dec 1 st at front slope edge **only** on every foll 6th row from previous dec until 31 [**35**, 39] sts rem.
Work straight until Left Front matches Back to start of shoulder shaping, ending with RS facing for next row.
Shape shoulder
Keeping patt correct, cast off 10 [**12**, 13] sts at beg of next and foll alt row. Work 1 row.
Cast off rem 11 [**11**, 13] sts.

RIGHT FRONT

With 5 mm (USA 8) needles, cast on 46 [**50**, 54] sts.
Rib patt thus:
Row 1 - (RS), (K1 tbl) 10 times, *P4, (K1 tbl) 4 times; rep from * to last 4 [**0**, 4] sts, P4 [**0**, 4].
Row 2 - K4 [**0**, 4], *(P1 tbl) 4 times, K4; rep from * to last 10 sts, (P1 tbl) 10 times.
These 2 rows form rib patt.
Patt a further 8 rows, thus ending with RS facing for next row.
Change to 5½ mm (USA 9) needles and work in rib patt for a further 20 rows, thus ending with RS facing for next row.
Shape side seam
Cont in rib patt, shaping side seams by inc 1 st at end of next and foll 20th row, taking inc sts into patt (48 [**52**, 56] sts).
Patt 19 rows, thus ending with RS facing for next row.
Place pocket
Next row - (RS), patt 10, slip next 28 sts onto a spare needle and, in their place, patt across 28 sts of second Pocket Lining, patt 9 [**13**, 17], inc in last st (49 [**53**, 57] sts).
Patt 19 rows, thus ending with RS facing for next row.

Inc 1 st at end of next row (50 [**54**, 58] sts).
Work straight until 8 rows less have been worked than on Back to start of armhole shaping, ending with RS facing for next row.
Shape front slope
Next row - (RS), (K1 tbl) 3 times, K2tog, patt to end (49 [**53**, 57] sts).
Working all front slope decreases as set by last row, complete to match Left Front, reversing shapings, working an extra row before start of armhole and shoulder shaping.

SLEEVES

With 5 mm (USA 8) needles, cast on 56 sts.
Row 1 - (RS), (K1 tbl) twice, *(P1 tbl) 4 times, (K1 tbl) 4 times; rep from * to last 6 sts, (P1 tbl) 4 times, (K1 tbl) twice.
Row 2 - (P1 tbl) twice, *(K1 tbl) 4 times, (P1 tbl) 4 times; rep from * to last 6 sts, (K1 tbl) 4 times, (P1 tbl) twice.
Rep last 2 rows 9 times more, thus ending with RS facing for next row.
Change to 5½ mm (USA 9) needles and **rib patt** thus:
Row 1 - (RS), (K1 tbl) twice, M1 (**by picking up horizontal loop lying before next st and working into back of it**), *P4, (K1 tbl) 4 times; rep from * to last 6 sts, P4, M1, (K1 tbl) twice (58 sts).
Row 2 - (P1 tbl) 3 times, *K4, (P1 tbl) 4 times; rep from * to last 7 sts, K4, (P1 tbl) 3 times.
These 2 rows form rib patt and set sleeve shaping.
Next row - (RS), (K1 tbl) twice, M1, patt to last 2 sts, M1, (K1 tbl) twice (60 sts).
Working all increases as set by last row, proceed thus:
Cont in rib patt, shaping sides by inc 1 st at each end of every foll alt row from previous inc to 66 [**72**, 80] sts, then on every foll 4th row until there are 96 [**100**, 104] sts, taking inc sts into rib patt.
Work straight until Sleeve meas 51 [**52**, 52] cm, ending with RS facing for next row.
Shape top
Keeping patt correct, cast off 4 sts at beg of next 2 rows (88 [**92**, 96] sts).
Dec 1 st at each end of next and foll 4 alt rows (78 [**82**, 86] sts).
Dec 1 st at each end of next row, thus ending with RS facing for next row.
Cast off rem 76 [**80**, 84] sts in patt.

MAKE UP

Pin out pieces to measurements given and steam press firmly to set rib. Allow to dry naturally before completing make up.
Join both shoulder seams.
Front Border
With 5 mm (USA 8) needles, cast on 22 sts.
Row 1 - (RS), K6, slip next st purlways with yarn at back of work (to form fold line), *(K1 tbl) twice, (P1 tbl) twice; rep from * twice more, (K1 tbl) twice, K1.

Row 2 - K1, (P1 tbl) twice, *(K1 tbl) twice, (P1 tbl) twice; rep from * twice more, P6, K1.

Noting to sew Border to garment with WS of Border facing RS of garment, rep last 2 rows until Border, when slightly stretched, fits up Right Front opening edge to start of front slope shaping, up right front slope, across back neck, down left front slope and then down to lower edge of Left Front, sewing in place as you go along and ending with RS facing for next row. Cast off in patt.

Fold Border back onto RS of garment along fold line and loosely stitch in place.

Pocket Tops
Slip 28 sts left on spare needle onto 5 mm (USA 8) needles and rejoin yarn with RS facing.

Work 2 rows in rib patt as set. Cast off loosely in patt.

Sew Pocket Linings in place on inside and sew down ends of Pocket Tops.

Place centre of cast-off edge of Sleeves to shoulder seams, then sew Sleeves into armholes, matching shaped edges. Join side and sleeve seams, leaving side seams open for lower 15 cm for side slit openings and reversing sleeve seam for first 7 cm for turn back cuff. Fold 5 cm cuff to RS.

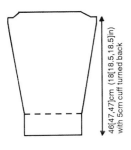

60[64.5,69]cm (23.5[25.5,27.25]in)

91[92,93]cm (36[36,36.5]in)

46[47,47]cm (18[18.5,18.5]in) with 5cm cuff turned back

Design 15

Bluster

To fit chest/bust											
61	**66**	71	**76**	81	**86**	91	**97**	102	**107**	112	cm
24	**26**	28	**30**	32	**34**	36	**38**	40	**42**	44	in
Actual size											
76	**82**	88	**95**	101	**107**	114	**120**	126	**133**	139	cm
30	**32**½	34½	**37**½	40	**42**	45	**47**	49½	**52**½	54½	in
Finished length											
39	**42**	45	**48**	57	**66**	68	**69**	71	**72**	73	cm
15½	**16**½	17½	**19**	22½	**26**	27	**27**	28	**28**½	28½	in
Sleeve length to underarm											
33	**36**	39	**42**	44	**46**	46	**48**	50	**52**	52	cm
13	**14**	15½	**16**½	17½	**18**	18	**19**	19½	**20**½	20½	in
Jaeger Matchmaker Merino Aran (799)											
8	**9**	10	**11**	13	**15**	17	**18**	19	**20**	22	50 gm
Jaeger Shetland Aran (031)											
4	**4**	5	**6**	6	**7**	8	**8**	9	**9**	10	100 gm

Quantities of yarn are approximate as they are based on average requirements. Check actual yarn colour - as printing may not match yarn exactly.

Pair each of 4 mm (UK 8/USA 6) and 4½ mm (UK 7/USA 7) needles.

Tension
19 sts and 32 rows to 10 cm (moss st), 19 sts and 25 rows to 10 cm (stocking st) on 4½ mm (USA 7) needles or size needed to achieve stated tension.

For notes and abbreviations, see page 58.

BACK
With 4 mm (USA 6) needles, cast on 74 [**78**, 86, **90**, 98, **102**, 110, **114**, 122, **126**, 134] sts. Starting with a K row, work in stocking st for 6 rows, thus ending with RS facing for next row.

Rib row 1 - (RS), K2, *P2, K2; rep from * to end.
Rib row 2 - P2, *K2, P2; rep from * to end.
61, 71, 81, 91, 102 and 112 cm sizes: Rep last 2 rows 3 times more, dec 1 st at each end of last row and thus ending with RS facing for next row (72 [84, 96, 108, 120, 132] sts).
66, 76, 86, 97 and 107 cm sizes: Rep last 2 rows 3 times more, thus ending with RS facing for next row.
All sizes: Change to 4½ mm (USA 7) needles.
Starting with a K row, work in stocking st until Back meas 21 [**23**, 25, **27**, 35, **43**, 44, **45**, 46, **47**, 47] cm, ending with RS facing for next row. (**Note**: Allow stocking st at lower edge to roll to RS before measuring.)
Shape armholes
Next row - (RS), cast off 4 [**4**, 4, **4**, 6, **6**, 6, **6**, 6, **6**, 6] sts (one st on right needle after cast off), P1, *K1, P1; rep from * to end.

49

Next row - Cast off 4 [**4**, 4, **4**, 6, **6**, 6, **6**, 6, **6**, 6] sts (one st on right needle after cast off), K1, *P1, K1; rep from * to end (64 [**70**, 76, **82**, 84, **90**, 96, **102**, 108, **114**, 120] sts).
Last 2 rows form moss st.
Cont in moss st until armhole meas 18 [**19**, 20, **21**, 22, **23**, 24, **24**, 25, **25**, 26] cm, ending with RS facing for next row.

Shape shoulders and back neck
Keeping patt correct, cast off 7 [**8**, 8, **9**, 10, **11**, 11, **12**, 13, **14**, 15] sts at beg of next 2 rows (50 [**54**, 60, **64**, 64, **68**, 74, **78**, 82, **86**, 90] sts).
Next row - (RS), cast off 7 [**8**, 8, **9**, 10, **11**, 11, **12**, 13, **14**, 15] sts, patt until there are 10 [**11**, 13, **14**, 12, **13**, 15, **16**, 16, **17**, 17] sts on right needle, turn and work this side first.
Cast off 4 sts at beg of next row.
Cast off rem 6 [**7**, 9, **10**, 8, **9**, 11, **12**, 12, **13**, 13] sts.
With RS facing, slip centre 16 [**16**, 18, **18**, 20, **20**, 22, **22**, 24, **24**, 26] sts onto a spare needle, rejoin yarn to rem sts, patt to end. Work to match first side, reversing shapings.

FRONT
Work as Back until 14 [**14**, 14, **16**, 16, **16**, 18, **18**, 18, **20**, 20] rows less have been worked before start of shoulder and back neck shaping, thus ending with RS facing for next row.

Shape front neck
Next row - (RS), patt 28 [**31**, 33, **36**, 36, **39**, 41, **44**, 46, **49**, 51], turn and work this side first.
Cast off 4 sts at beg of next row (24 [**27**, 29, **32**, 32, **35**, 37, **40**, 42, **45**, 47] sts). Dec 1 st at neck edge on next 2 rows, then on foll 2 alt rows (20 [**23**, 25, **28**, 28, **31**, 33, **36**, 38, **41**, 43] sts). Work 6 [**6**, 6, **8**, 8, **8**, 10, **10**, 10, **12**, 12] rows, thus ending with RS facing for next row.

Shape shoulder
Cast off 7 [**8**, 8, **9**, 10, **11**, 11, **12**, 13, **14**, 15] sts at beg of next and foll alt row. Work 1 row.
Cast off rem 6 [**7**, 9, **10**, 8, **9**, 11, **12**, 12, **13**, 13] sts.
With RS facing, slip centre 8 [**8**, 10, **10**, 12, **12**, 14, **14**, 16, **16**, 18] sts onto a spare needle, rejoin yarn to rem sts, patt to end. Work to match first side, reversing shapings, working an extra row before start of shoulder shaping.

SLEEVES
With 4 mm (USA 6) needles, cast on 38 [**38**, 42, **42**, 46, **46**, 50, **50**, 54, **54**, 58] sts.
Starting with a K row, work in stocking st for 6 rows, thus ending with RS facing for next row.
Starting with rib row 1, work in rib as for Back for 8 rows, ending with RS facing for next row.
Change to 4½ mm (USA 7) needles and starting with a K row, work in stocking st, shaping sides by inc 1 st at each end of next and every foll 4th row to 56 [**62**, 60, **64**, 64, **74**, 78, **72**, 72, **66**, 70] sts, then on every foll 6th row until there are 66 [**70**, 74, **78**, 82, **86**, 90, **90**, 94, **94**, 98] sts.

Work straight until Sleeve meas 33 [**36**, 39, **42**, 44, **46**, 46, **48**, 50, **52**, 52] cm, ending with RS facing for next row. (**Note**: Allow stocking st at lower edge to roll to RS before measuring.)
Shape top
Place markers at both ends of last row to denote top of sleeve seam.
Work a further 5 [**5**, 5, **5**, 8, **8**, 8, **8**, 8, **8**, 8] rows. Cast off loosely.

MAKE UP
Press carefully following instructions on ball band.
Join right shoulder seam.
Neck Border
With RS facing and 4 mm (USA 6) needles, **knit up** 17 [**17**, 17, **19**, 19, **19**, 21, **21**, 21, **23**, 23] sts down left side of front neck, K 8 [**8**, 10, **10**, 12, **12**, 14, **14**, 16, **16**, 18] sts from Front, **knit up** 17 [**17**, 17, **19**, 19, **19**, 21, **21**, 21, **23**, 23] sts up right side of front neck, 4 sts down right side of back neck, K 16 [**16**, 18, **18**, 20, **20**, 22, **22**, 24, **24**, 26] sts from Back, then **knit up** 4 sts up left side of back neck (66 [**66**, 70, **74**, 78, **78**, 86, **86**, 90, **94**, 98] sts).
Starting with rib row 2, work in rib as for Back for 7 rows, thus ending with RS facing for next row.
Change to 4½ mm (USA 7) needles and starting with a K row, work in stocking st for 6 rows.
Cast off loosely.
Join left shoulder seam and Neck Border, reversing seam for stocking st roll.
Place centre of cast-off edge of Sleeves to shoulder seams, then sew Sleeves into armholes, matching sleeve markers to top of side seams. Join side and sleeve seams, reversing seams for stocking st rolls.

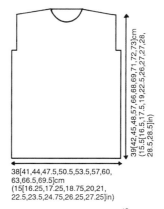

38[41,44,47.5,50.5,53.5,57,60,
63,66.5,69.5]cm
(15[16.25,17.25,18.75,20,21,
22.5,23.5,24.75,26.25,27.25]in)

39[42,45,48,57,66,68,69,71,72,73]cm
(15.5[16.5,17.5,19,22.5,26,27,27,28,
28.5,28.5]in)

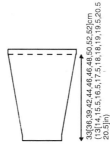

33[36,39,42,44,46,46,48,50,52,52]cm
(13[14,15.5,16.5,17.5,18,18,19,19.5,20.5,
20.5]in)

Design 16

Hush

To fit bust					
81	**86**	91	**97**	102	cm
32	**34**	36	**38**	40	in
Actual size					
113	**117**	123	**127**	133	cm
44½	**46**	48½	**50**	52½	in
Finished length					
71	**71**	72	**72**	73	cm
28	**28**	28½	**28½**	28½	in
Sleeve length to underarm					
47	**47**	48	**48**	48	cm
18½	**18½**	19	**19**	19	in
Jaeger Matchmaker Merino Aran (662)					
18	**18**	19	**20**	21	50 gm
Jaeger Shetland Aran					
9	**9**	10	**11**	11	100 gm

Quantities of yarn are approximate as they are based on average requirements. Check actual yarn colour - as printing may not match yarn exactly.

Pair each of 4 mm (UK 8/USA 6) and 4½ mm (UK 7/USA 7) needles.

Tension
20 sts and 25 rows to 10 cm (patt), 19 sts and 25 rows to 10 cm (stocking st) on 4½ mm (USA 7) needles or size needed to achieve stated tension.

For notes and abbreviations, see page 58.

BACK
With 4 mm (USA 6) needles, cast on 113 [**117**, 123, **127**, 133] sts.
Rib row 1 - (RS), K0 [**1**, 4, **0**, 0], P4 [**5**, 5, **1**, 4], *K5, P5; rep from * to last 9 [**1**, 4, **6**, 9] sts, K5 [**1**, 4, **5**, 5], P4 [**0**, 0, **1**, 4].

Rib row 2 - P0 [**1**, 4, **0**, 0], K4 [**5**, 5, **1**, 4], *P5, K5; rep from * to last 9 [**1**, 4, **6**, 9] sts, P5 [**1**, 4, **5**, 5], K4 [**0**, 0, **1**, 4].

Rep last 2 rows 9 times more, thus ending with RS facing for next row.

Change to 4½ mm (USA 7) needles and starting and ending rows at points indicated, work in patt foll chart, repeating the 40 row patt repeat throughout, until Back meas 48 cm, ending with RS facing for next row.

Shape armholes

Keeping patt correct, cast off 6 sts at beg of next 2 rows (101 [**105**, 111, **115**, 121] sts).

Work straight until armhole meas 23 [**23**, 24, **24**, 25] cm, ending with RS facing for next row.

Shape shoulders and back neck

Keeping patt correct, cast off 11 [**12**, 13, **14**, 15] sts at beg of next 2 rows
(79 [**81**, 85, **87**, 91] sts).

Next row - (RS), cast off 11 [**12**, 13, **14**, 15] sts, patt until there are 16 [**16**, 17, **17**, 18] sts on right needle, turn and work this side first.

Cast off 4 sts at beg of next row.

Cast off rem 12 [**12**, 13, **13**, 14] sts.

With RS facing, slip centre 25 sts onto a spare needle, rejoin yarn to rem sts, patt to end.

Work to match first side, reversing shapings.

FRONT

Work as Back until 18 rows less have been worked before start of shoulder and back neck shaping, thus ending with RS facing for next row.

Shape front neck

Next row - (RS), patt 42 [**44**, 47, **49**, 52], turn and work this side first.

Cast off 3 sts at beg of next row
(39 [**41**, 44, **46**, 49] sts).

Dec 1 st at neck edge on next 2 rows, then on foll 2 alt rows
(35 [**37**, 40, **42**, 45] sts).

Work 3 rows.

Dec 1 st at neck edge on next row
(34 [**36**, 39, **41**, 44] sts).

Work 6 rows, thus ending with RS facing for next row.

Shape shoulder

Cast off 11 [**12**, 13, **14**, 15] sts at beg of next and foll alt row.

Work 1 row.

Cast off rem 12 [**12**, 13, **13**, 14] sts.

With RS facing, slip centre 17 sts onto a spare needle, rejoin yarn to rem sts, patt to end.

Work to match first side, reversing shapings, working an extra row before start of shoulder shaping.

SLEEVES

With 4 mm (USA 6) needles, cast on 55 sts.

Rib row 1 - (RS), P5, *K5, P5; rep from * to end.

Rib row 2 - K5, *P5, K5; rep from * to end.

Rep last 2 rows 9 times more, thus ending with RS facing for next row.

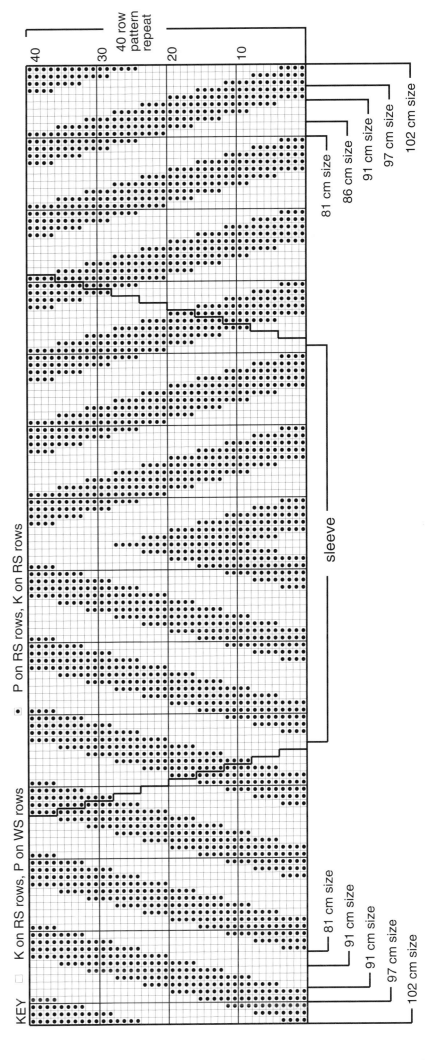

51

Change to 4¹/₂ mm (USA 7) needles and starting and ending rows at points indicated, work in patt foll chart, repeating the 40 row patt repeat throughout, shaping sides by inc 1 st at each end of chart row 1 and every foll 4th row until there are 85 [**85**, 93, **93**, 101] sts, taking inc sts into patt.

81, 86, 91 and 97 cm sizes: Inc 1 st at each end of every foll 6th row from previous inc until there are 93 [**93**, 97, **97**] sts.

All sizes:
Work straight until Sleeve meas 47 [**47**, 48, **48**, 48] cm, ending with RS facing for next row.

Shape top
Place markers at both ends of last row to denote top of sleeve seam.
Work a further 8 rows, thus ending with RS facing for next row.
Cast off loosely and evenly in rib patt.

MAKE UP

Pin out pieces to measurements given and steam press firmly to set patt. Allow to dry naturally before completing make up.
Join right shoulder seam.

Neck Border

With RS facing and 4 mm (USA 6) needles, **knit up** 20 sts down left side of front neck, patt 17 sts from Front, **knit up** 20 sts up right side of front neck, 4 sts down right side of back neck, patt 25 sts from Back, then **knit up** 4 sts up left side of back neck (90 sts).
Row 1 - (WS), *K5, P5; rep from * to end.
Rep last row until Neck Border meas 10 cm.
Cast off loosely in patt.
Join left shoulder seam and Neck Border.
Place centre of cast-off edge of Sleeves to shoulder seams, then sew Sleeves into armholes, matching sleeve markers to top of side seams. Join side and sleeve seams.

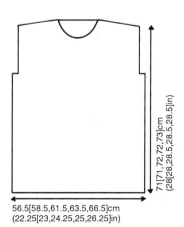

56.5[58.5,61.5,63.5,66.5]cm
(22.25[23,24.25,25,26.25]in)

71[71,72,72,73]cm
(28[28,28.5,28.5,28.5]in)

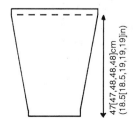

47[47,48,48,48]cm
(18.5[18.5,19,19,19]in)

Maple Throw and Chevron Cushions

Design 17

Chevron Cushions

Actual size

45	x	45	cm
17¹/₂	x	17¹/₂	in

DK Version
Jaeger Matchmaker Merino DK (782)
　　3　　50 gm
4 Ply Version
Jaeger Cashmere 4 Ply (116)
　　3　　25 gm
Quantities of yarn are approximate as they are based on average requirements. Check actual yarn colour - as printing may not match yarn exactly.

DK Cushion: Pair of 4 mm (UK 8/USA 6) needles.
4 Ply Cushion: Pair of 3¹/₄ mm (UK 10/USA 3) needles.
DK or 4 Ply Cushion: 45 cm (17¹/₂ in) cushion pad and cover.

Tension
DK Cushion: 24 sts and 30 rows to 10 cm (stocking st) on 4 mm (USA 6) needles or size needed to achieve stated tension.
4 Ply Cushion: 28 sts and 36 rows to 10 cm (stocking st) on 3¹/₄ mm (USA 3) needles or size needed to achieve stated tension.

For notes and abbreviations, see page 58.

DK CUSHION

With 4 mm (USA 6) needles, cast on 99 sts.
Now work in textured patt following chart, starting and ending rows at points indicated and repeating the 36 st patt repeat twice across rows.
Cont in patt, repeating the 24 patt rows throughout, until Cushion meas 45 cm, ending with RS facing for next row. Cast off in patt.

4 PLY CUSHION

With 3¹/₄ mm (USA 3) needles, cast on 127 sts.
Now work in textured patt following chart, starting and ending rows at points indicated and repeating the 36 st patt repeat twice across rows.
Cont in patt, repeating the 24 patt rows throughout, until Cushion meas 45 cm, ending with RS facing for next row. Cast off in patt.

MAKE UP

Press carefully following instructions on ball band. Carefully stitch knitted panel to front of cushion cover.